The Psychology of Money

The Psychology *of* Money

TIMELESS LESSONS ON WEALTH, GREED,
AND HAPPINESS

MORGAN HOUSEL

Published in arrangement with
Harriman House Ltd.
3 Viceroy Court, Bedford Road
Petersfield, Hampshire, GU32 3LJ
United Kingdom
harriman-house.com

Originally published in the UK by
Harriman House Ltd in 2020
www.harriman-house.com

THE PSYCHOLOGY OF MONEY
ISBN 978-93-90166-26-8

First Jaico Impression: 2020
Sixth Jaico Impression: 2020

For

My parents, who teach me.

Gretchen, who guides me.

Miles and Reese, who inspire me.

Contents

"A genius is the man who can do the average thing when everyone else around him is losing his mind."

—Napoleon

"The world is full of obvious things which nobody by any chance ever observes."

—Sherlock Holmes

INTRODUCTION: The Greatest Show On Earth

I SPENT MY COLLEGE years working as a valet at a nice hotel in Los Angeles.

One frequent guest was a technology executive. He was a genius, having designed and patented a key component in Wi-Fi routers in his 20s. He had started and sold several companies. He was wildly successful.

He also had a relationship with money I'd describe as a mix of insecurity and childish stupidity.

He carried a stack of hundred dollar bills several inches thick. He showed it to everyone who wanted to see it and many who didn't. He bragged openly and loudly about his wealth, often while drunk and always apropos of nothing.

One day he handed one of my colleagues several thousand dollars of cash and said, "Go to the jewelry store down the street and get me a few $1,000 gold coins."

An hour later, gold coins in hand, the tech executive and his buddies gathered around by a dock overlooking the Pacific Ocean. They then proceeded to throw the coins into the sea, skipping them like rocks, cackling as they argued whose went furthest. Just for fun.

Days later he shattered a lamp in the hotel's restaurant. A manager told him it was a $500 lamp and he'd have to replace it.

"You want five hundred dollars?" the executive asked incredulously, while pulling a brick of cash from his pocket and handing it to the manager. "Here's five thousand dollars. Now get out of my face. And don't ever insult me like that again."

You may wonder how long this behavior could last, and the answer was "not long." I learned years later that he went broke.

The premise of this book is that doing well with money has a little to do with how smart you are and a lot to do with how you behave. And behavior is hard to teach, even to really smart people.

A genius who loses control of their emotions can be a financial disaster. The opposite is also true. Ordinary folks with no financial education can be wealthy if they have a handful of behavioral skills that have nothing to do with formal measures of intelligence.

My favorite Wikipedia entry begins: "Ronald James Read was an American philanthropist, investor, janitor, and gas station attendant."

Ronald Read was born in rural Vermont. He was the first person in his family to graduate high school, made all the more impressive by the fact that he hitchhiked to campus each day.

For those who knew Ronald Read, there wasn't much else worth mentioning. His life was about as low key as they come.

Read fixed cars at a gas station for 25 years and swept floors at JCPenney for 17 years. He bought a two-bedroom house for $12,000 at age 38 and lived there for the rest of his life. He was widowed at age 50 and never remarried. A friend recalled that his main hobby was chopping firewood.

Read died in 2014, age 92. Which is when the humble rural janitor made international headlines.

2,813,503 Americans died in 2014. Fewer than 4,000 of them had a net worth of over $8 million when they passed away. Ronald Read was one of them.

In his will the former janitor left $2 million to his stepkids and more than $6 million to his local hospital and library.

Those who knew Read were baffled. Where did he get all that money?

It turned out there was no secret. There was no lottery win and no inheritance. Read saved what little he could and invested it in blue chip stocks. Then he waited, for decades on end, as tiny savings compounded into more than $8 million.

That's it. From janitor to philanthropist.

A few months before Ronald Read died, another man named Richard was in the news.

Richard Fuscone was everything Ronald Read was not. A Harvard-educated Merrill Lynch executive with an MBA, Fuscone had such a successful career in finance that he retired in his 40s to become a philanthropist. Former Merrill CEO David Komansky praised Fuscone's "business savvy, leadership skills, sound judgment and personal integrity."[1] *Crain's* business magazine once included him in a "40 under 40" list of successful businesspeople.[2]

But then—like the gold-coin-skipping tech executive—everything fell apart.

In the mid-2000s Fuscone borrowed heavily to expand an 18,000-square foot home in Greenwich, Connecticut that had 11 bathrooms, two elevators, two pools, seven garages, and cost more than $90,000 a month to maintain.

Then the 2008 financial crisis hit.

The crisis hurt virtually everyone's finances. It apparently turned Fuscone's into dust. High debt and illiquid assets left him bankrupt. "I currently have no income," he allegedly told a bankruptcy judge in 2008.

First his Palm Beach house was foreclosed.

In 2014 it was the Greenwich mansion's turn.

Five months before Ronald Read left his fortune to charity,

Richard Fuscone's home—where guests recalled the "thrill of dining and dancing atop a see-through covering on the home's indoor swimming pool"—was sold in a foreclosure auction for 75% less than an insurance company figured it was worth.[3]

Ronald Read was patient; Richard Fuscone was greedy. That's all it took to eclipse the massive education and experience gap between the two.

The lesson here is not to be more like Ronald and less like Richard—though that's not bad advice.

The fascinating thing about these stories is how unique they are to finance.

In what other industry does someone with no college degree, no training, no background, no formal experience, and no connections massively outperform someone with the best education, the best training, and the best connections?

I struggle to think of any.

It is impossible to think of a story about Ronald Read performing a heart transplant better than a Harvard-trained surgeon. Or designing a skyscraper superior to the best-trained architects. There will never be a story of a janitor outperforming the world's top nuclear engineers.

But these stories do happen in investing.

The fact that Ronald Read can coexist with Richard Fuscone has two explanations. One, financial outcomes are driven by luck, independent of intelligence and effort. That's true to some extent, and this book will discuss it in further detail. Or, two (and I think more common), that financial success is not a hard science. It's a soft skill, where how you behave is more important than what you know.

I call this soft skill the psychology of money. The aim of this book is to use short stories to convince you that soft skills are more important than the technical side of money. I'll do this in a way that will help everyone—from Read to Fuscone and everyone in between—make better financial decisions.

These soft skills are, I've come to realize, greatly underappreciated. Finance is overwhelmingly taught as a math-based field, where you put data into a formula and the formula tells you what to do, and it's assumed that you'll just go do it.

This is true in personal finance, where you're told to have a six-month emergency fund and save 10% of your salary.

It's true in investing, where we know the exact historical correlations between interest rates and valuations.

And it's true in corporate finance, where CFOs can measure the precise cost of capital.

It's not that any of these things are bad or wrong. It's that knowing what to do tells you nothing about what happens in your head when you try to do it.

Two topics impact everyone, whether you are interested in them or not: health and money.

The health care industry is a triumph of modern science, with rising life expectancy across the world. Scientific discoveries have replaced doctors' old ideas about how the human body works, and virtually everyone is healthier because of it.

The money industry—investing, personal finance, business planning—is another story.

Finance has scooped up the smartest minds coming from top universities over the last two decades. Financial Engineering was the most popular major in Princeton's School of Engineering a decade ago. Is there any evidence it has made us better investors?

I have seen none.

Through collective trial and error over the years we learned how to become better farmers, skilled plumbers, and advanced chemists. But has trial and error taught us to become better with our personal finances? Are we less likely to bury ourselves in debt? More likely to save for a rainy day? Prepare for retirement?

Have realistic views about what money does, and doesn't do, to our happiness?

I've seen no compelling evidence.

Most of the reason why, I believe, is that we think about and are taught about money in ways that are too much like physics (with rules and laws) and not enough like psychology (with emotions and nuance).

And that, to me, is as fascinating as it is important.

Money is everywhere, it affects all of us, and confuses most of us. Everyone thinks about it a little differently. It offers lessons on things that apply to many areas of life, like risk, confidence, and happiness. Few topics offer a more powerful magnifying glass that helps explain why people behave the way they do than money. It is one of the greatest shows on Earth.

My own appreciation for the psychology of money is shaped by more than a decade of writing on the topic. I began writing about finance in early 2008. It was the dawn of a financial crisis and the worst recession in 80 years.

To write about what was happening, I wanted to figure out what was happening. But the first thing I learned after the financial crisis was that no one could accurately explain what happened, or why it happened, let alone what should be done about it. For every good explanation there was an equally convincing rebuttal.

Engineers can determine the cause of a bridge collapse because there's agreement that if a certain amount of force is applied to a certain area, that area will break. Physics isn't controversial. It's guided by laws. Finance is different. It's guided by people's behaviors. And how I behave might make sense to me but look crazy to you.

The more I studied and wrote about the financial crisis, the more I realized that you could understand it better through the lenses of psychology and history, not finance.

To grasp why people bury themselves in debt you don't need

to study interest rates; you need to study the history of greed, insecurity, and optimism. To get why investors sell out at the bottom of a bear market you don't need to study the math of expected future returns; you need to think about the agony of looking at your family and wondering if your investments are imperiling their future.

I love Voltaire's observation that "History never repeats itself; man always does." It applies so well to how we behave with money.

In 2018, I wrote a report outlining 20 of the most important flaws, biases, and causes of bad behavior I've seen affect people when dealing with money. It was called The Psychology of Money, and over one million people have read it. This book is a deeper dive into the topic. Some short passages from the report appear unaltered in this book.

What you're holding is 20 chapters, each describing what I consider to be the most important and often counterintuitive features of the psychology of money. The chapters revolve around a common theme, but exist on their own and can be read independently.

It's not a long book. You're welcome. Most readers don't finish the books they begin because most single topics don't require 300 pages of explanation. I'd rather make 20 short points you finish than one long one you give up on.

On we go.

1.

No One's Crazy

Your personal experiences with money make up maybe 0.00000001% of what's happened in the world, but maybe 80% of how you think the world works.

LET ME TELL you about a problem. It might make you feel better about what you do with your money, and less judgmental about what other people do with theirs.

People do some crazy things with money. But no one is crazy.

Here's the thing: People from different generations, raised by different parents who earned different incomes and held different values, in different parts of the world, born into different economies, experiencing different job markets with different incentives and different degrees of luck, learn very different lessons.

Everyone has their own unique experience with how the world works. And what you've experienced is more compelling than what you learn second-hand. So all of us—you, me, everyone—go through life anchored to a set of views about how money works that vary wildly from person to person. What seems crazy to you might make sense to me.

The person who grew up in poverty thinks about risk and reward in ways the child of a wealthy banker cannot fathom if he tried.

The person who grew up when inflation was high experienced something the person who grew up with stable prices never had to.

The stock broker who lost everything during the Great Depression experienced something the tech worker basking in the glory of the late 1990s can't imagine.

The Australian who hasn't seen a recession in 30 years has experienced something no American ever has.

On and on. The list of experiences is endless.

You know stuff about money that I don't, and vice versa. You go through life with different beliefs, goals, and forecasts, than I do. That's not because one of us is smarter than the other, or has better information. It's because we've had different lives shaped by different and equally persuasive experiences.

Your personal experiences with money make up maybe 0.00000001% of what's happened in the world, but maybe 80% of how you think the world works. So equally smart people can disagree about how and why recessions happen, how you should invest your money, what you should prioritize, how much risk you should take, and so on.

In his book on 1930s America, Frederick Lewis Allen wrote that the Great Depression "marked millions of Americans—inwardly—for the rest of their lives." But there was a range of experiences. Twenty-five years later, as he was running for president, John F. Kennedy was asked by a reporter what he remembered from the Depression. He remarked:

> I have no first-hand knowledge of the Depression. My family had one of the great fortunes of the world and it was worth more than ever then. We had bigger houses, more servants, we traveled more. About the only thing that I saw directly was when my father hired some extra gardeners just to give them a job so they could eat. I really did not learn about the Depression until I read about it at Harvard.

This was a major point in the 1960 election. How, people thought, could someone with no understanding of the biggest economic story of the last generation be put in charge of the economy? It was, in many ways, overcome only by JFK's experience in World War II. That was the other most widespread emotional experience of the previous generation, and something his primary opponent, Hubert Humphrey, didn't have.

The challenge for us is that no amount of studying or open-mindedness can genuinely recreate the power of fear and uncertainty.

I can read about what it was like to lose everything during the Great Depression. But I don't have the emotional scars of those who actually experienced it. And the person who lived through it can't fathom why someone like me could come across as complacent about things like owning stocks. We see the world through a different lens.

Spreadsheets can model the historic frequency of big stock market declines. But they can't model the feeling of coming home, looking at your kids, and wondering if you've made a mistake that will impact their lives. Studying history makes you feel like you understand something. But until you've lived through it and personally felt its consequences, you may not understand it enough to change your behavior.

We all think we know how the world works. But we've all only experienced a tiny sliver of it.

As investor Michael Batnick says, "some lessons have to be experienced before they can be understood." We are all victims, in different ways, to that truth.

In 2006 economists Ulrike Malmendier and Stefan Nagel from the National Bureau of Economic Research dug through 50 years of the Survey of Consumer Finances—a detailed look at what Americans do with their money.[4]

In theory people should make investment decisions based on their goals and the characteristics of the investment options available to them at the time.

But that's not what people do.

The economists found that people's lifetime investment decisions are heavily anchored to the experiences those investors had in their own generation—especially experiences early in their adult life.

If you grew up when inflation was high, you invested less of your money in bonds later in life compared to those who grew up when inflation was low. If you happened to grow up when the stock market was strong, you invested more of your money in stocks later in life compared to those who grew up when stocks were weak.

The economists wrote: "Our findings suggest that individual investors' willingness to bear risk depends on personal history."

Not intelligence, or education, or sophistication. Just the dumb luck of when and where you were born.

The *Financial Times* interviewed Bill Gross, the famed bond manager, in 2019. "Gross admits that he would probably not be where he is today if he had been born a decade earlier or later," the piece said. Gross's career coincided almost perfectly with a generational collapse in interest rates that gave bond prices a tailwind. That kind of thing doesn't just affect the opportunities you come across; it affects what you think about those opportunities when they're presented to you. To Gross, bonds were wealth-generating machines. To his father's generation, who grew up with and endured higher inflation, they might be seen as wealth incinerators.

The differences in how people have experienced money are not small, even among those you might think are pretty similar.

Take stocks. If you were born in 1970, the S&P 500 increased almost 10-fold, adjusted for inflation, during your teens and 20s. That's an amazing return. If you were born in 1950, the market went literally nowhere in your teens and 20s adjusted for inflation. Two groups of people, separated by chance of their birth year, go through life with a completely different view on how the stock market works:

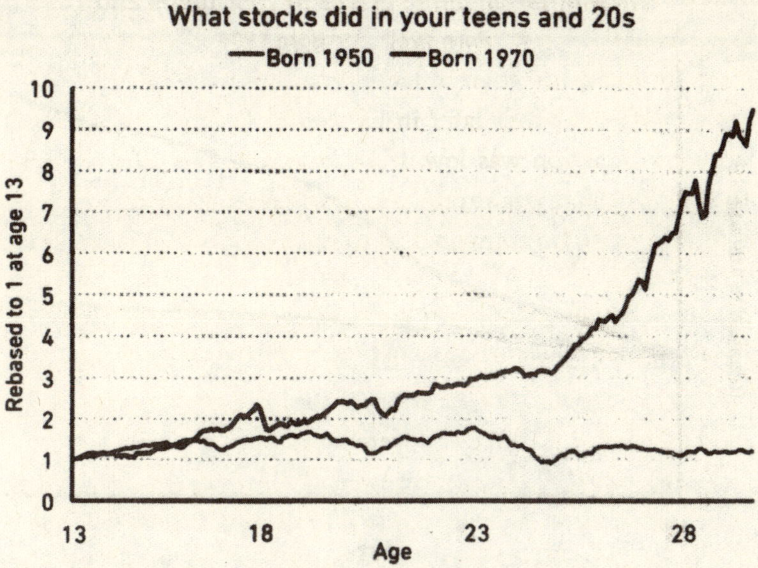

Or inflation. If you were born in 1960s America, inflation during your teens and 20s—your young, impressionable years when you're developing a base of knowledge about how the economy works—sent prices up more than threefold. That's a lot. You remember gas lines and getting paychecks that stretched noticeably less far than the ones before them. But if you were born in 1990, inflation has been so low for your whole life that it's probably never crossed your mind.

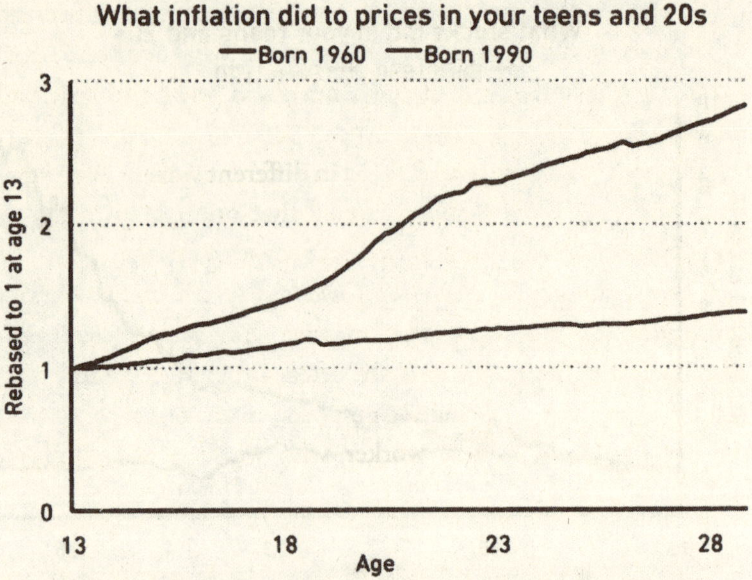

America's nationwide unemployment in November 2009 was around 10%. But the unemployment rate for African American males age 16 to 19 without a high school diploma was 49%. For Caucasian females over age 45 with a college degree, it was 4%.

Local stock markets in Germany and Japan were wiped out during World War II. Entire regions were bombed out. At the end of the war German farms only produced enough food to provide the country's citizens with 1,000 calories a day. Compare that to the U.S., where the stock market more than doubled from 1941 through the end of 1945, and the economy was the strongest it had been in almost two decades.

No one should expect members of these groups to go through the rest of their lives thinking the same thing about inflation. Or the stock market. Or unemployment. Or money in general.

No one should expect them to respond to financial information the same way. No one should assume they are influenced by the same incentives.

No one should expect them to trust the same sources of advice.

No one should expect them to agree on what matters, what's worth it, what's likely to happen next, and what the best path forward is.

Their view of money was formed in different worlds. And when that's the case, a view about money that one group of people thinks is outrageous can make perfect sense to another.

A few years ago, *The New York Times* did a story on the working conditions of Foxconn, the massive Taiwanese electronics manufacturer. The conditions are often atrocious. Readers were rightly upset. But a fascinating response to the story came from the nephew of a Chinese worker, who wrote in the comment section:

> My aunt worked several years in what Americans call "sweat shops." It was hard work. Long hours, "small" wage, "poor" working conditions. Do you know what my aunt did before she worked in one of these factories? She was a prostitute.
>
> The idea of working in a "sweat shop" compared to that old lifestyle is an improvement, in my opinion. I know that my aunt would rather be "exploited" by an evil capitalist boss for a couple of dollars than have her body be exploited by several men for pennies.
>
> That is why I am upset by many Americans' thinking. We do not have the same opportunities as the West. Our governmental infrastructure is different. The country is different. Yes, factory is hard labor. Could it be better? Yes, but only when you compare such to American jobs.

I don't know what to make of this. Part of me wants to argue, fiercely. Part of me wants to understand. But mostly it's an example of how different experiences can lead to vastly different views within topics that one side intuitively thinks should be black and white.

Every decision people make with money is justified by taking the information they have at the moment and plugging it into their unique mental model of how the world works.

Those people can be misinformed. They can have incomplete information. They can be bad at math. They can be persuaded by rotten marketing. They can have no idea what they're doing. They can misjudge the consequences of their actions. Oh, can they ever.

But every financial decision a person makes, makes sense to them in that moment and checks the boxes they need to check. They tell themselves a story about what they're doing and why they're doing it, and that story has been shaped by their own unique experiences.

Take a simple example: lottery tickets.

Americans spend more on them than movies, video games, music, sporting events, and books combined.

And who buys them? Mostly poor people.

The lowest-income households in the U.S. on average spend $412 a year on lotto tickets, four times the amount of those in the highest income groups. Forty percent of Americans cannot come up with $400 in an emergency. Which is to say: Those buying $400 in lottery tickets are by and large the same people who say they couldn't come up with $400 in an emergency. They are blowing their safety nets on something with a one-in-millions chance of hitting it big.

That seems crazy to me. It probably seems crazy to you, too. But I'm not in the lowest income group. You're likely not, either. So it's hard for many of us to intuitively grasp the subconscious reasoning of low-income lottery ticket buyers.

But strain a little, and you can imagine it going something like this:

> We live paycheck-to-paycheck and saving seems out of reach. Our prospects for much higher wages seem out of reach. We

> can't afford nice vacations, new cars, health insurance, or homes in safe neighborhoods. We can't put our kids through college without crippling debt. Much of the stuff you people who read finance books either have now, or have a good chance of getting, we don't. Buying a lottery ticket is the only time in our lives we can hold a tangible dream of getting the good stuff that you already have and take for granted. We are paying for a dream, and you may not understand that because you are already living a dream. That's why we buy more tickets than you do.

You don't have to agree with this reasoning. Buying lotto tickets when you're broke is still a bad idea. But I can kind of understand why lotto ticket sales persist.

And that idea—"What you're doing seems crazy but I kind of understand why you're doing it."—uncovers the root of many of our financial decisions.

Few people make financial decisions purely with a spreadsheet. They make them at the dinner table, or in a company meeting. Places where personal history, your own unique view of the world, ego, pride, marketing, and odd incentives are scrambled together into a narrative that works for you.

Another important point that helps explain why money decisions are so difficult, and why there is so much misbehavior, is to recognize how new this topic is.

Money has been around a long time. King Alyattes of Lydia, now part of Turkey, is thought to have created the first official currency in 600 BC. But the modern foundation of money decisions—saving and investing—is based around concepts that are practically infants.

Take retirement. At the end of 2018 there was $27 trillion in U.S. retirement accounts, making it the main driver of the common investor's saving and investing decisions.[5]

But the entire concept of being entitled to retirement is, at most, two generations old.

Before World War II most Americans worked until they died. That was the expectation and the reality. The labor force participation rate of men age 65 and over was above 50% until the 1940s:

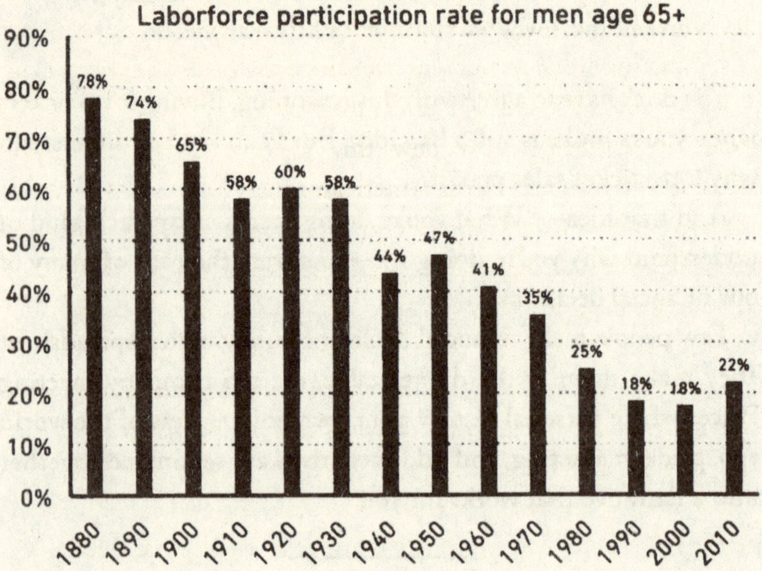

Social Security aimed to change this. But its initial benefits were nothing close to a proper pension. When Ida May Fuller cashed the first Social Security check in 1940, it was for $22.54, or $416 adjusted for inflation. It was not until the 1980s that the average Social Security check for retirees exceeded $1,000 a month adjusted for inflation. More than a quarter of Americans over age 65 were classified by the Census Bureau as living in poverty until the late 1960s.

There is a widespread belief along the lines of, "everyone used to have a private pension." But this is wildly exaggerated. The Employee Benefit Research Institute explains: "Only a quarter of those age 65 or older had pension income in 1975." Among that lucky minority, only 15% of household income came from a pension.

The New York Times wrote in 1955 about the growing desire, but continued inability, to retire: "To rephrase an old saying: everyone talks about retirement, but apparently very few do anything about it."[6]

It was not until the 1980s that the idea that everyone deserves, and should have, a dignified retirement took hold. And the way to get that dignified retirement ever since has been an expectation that everyone will save and invest their own money.

Let me reiterate how new this idea is: The 401(k)—the backbone savings vehicle of American retirement—did not exist until 1978. The Roth IRA was not born until 1998. If it were a person it would be barely old enough to drink.

It should surprise no one that many of us are bad at saving and investing for retirement. We're not crazy. We're all just newbies.

Same goes for college. The share of Americans over age 25 with a bachelor's degree has gone from less than 1 in 20 in 1940 to 1 in 4 by 2015.[7] The average college tuition over that time rose more than fourfold adjusted for inflation.[8] Something so big and so important hitting society so fast explains why, for example, so many people have made poor decisions with student loans over the last 20 years. There is not decades of accumulated experience to even attempt to learn from. We're winging it.

Same for index funds, which are less than 50 years old. And hedge funds, which didn't take off until the last 25 years. Even widespread use of consumer debt—mortgages, credit cards, and car loans—did not take off until after World War II, when the GI Bill made it easier for millions of Americans to borrow.

Dogs were domesticated 10,000 years ago and still retain some behaviors of their wild ancestors. Yet here we are, with between 20 and 50 years of experience in the modern financial system, hoping to be perfectly acclimated.

For a topic that is so influenced by emotion versus fact, this is a problem. And it helps explain why we don't always do what we're supposed to with money.

We all do crazy stuff with money, because we're all relatively new to this game and what looks crazy to you might make sense to me. But no one is crazy—we all make decisions based on our own unique experiences that seem to make sense to us in a given moment.

Now let me tell you a story about how Bill Gates got rich.

2.

Luck & Risk

Nothing is as good or as bad as it seems.

LUCK AND RISK are siblings. They are both the reality that every outcome in life is guided by forces other than individual effort.

NYU professor Scott Galloway has a related idea that is so important to remember when judging success—both your own and others': "Nothing is as good or as bad as it seems."

Bill Gates went to one of the only high schools in the world that had a computer.

The story of how Lakeside School, just outside Seattle, even got a computer is remarkable.

Bill Dougall was a World War II navy pilot turned high school math and science teacher. "He believed that book study wasn't enough without real-world experience. He also realized that we'd need to know something about computers when we got to college," recalled late Microsoft co-founder Paul Allen.

In 1968 Dougall petitioned the Lakeside School Mothers' Club to use the proceeds from its annual rummage sale—about $3,000—to lease a Teletype Model 30 computer hooked up to the General Electric mainframe terminal for computer time-sharing. "The whole idea of time-sharing only got invented in 1965," Gates later said. "Someone was pretty forwardlooking." Most university graduate schools did not have a computer anywhere near as advanced as Bill Gates had access to in eighth grade. And he couldn't get enough of it.

Gates was 13 years old in 1968 when he met classmate Paul Allen. Allen was also obsessed with the school's computer, and the two hit it off.

Lakeside's computer wasn't part of its general curriculum. It was an independent study program. Bill and Paul could toy away with the thing at their leisure, letting their creativity run wild—after school, late into the night, on weekends. They quickly became computing experts.

During one of their late-night sessions, Allen recalled Gates showing him a *Fortune* magazine and saying, "What do you think it's like to run a Fortune 500 company?" Allen said he had no idea. "Maybe we'll have our own computer company someday," Gates said. Microsoft is now worth more than a trillion dollars.

A little quick math.

In 1968 there were roughly 303 million high-school-age people in the world, according to the UN.

About 18 million of them lived in the United States.

About 270,000 of them lived in Washington state.

A little over 100,000 of them lived in the Seattle area.

And only about 300 of them attended Lakeside School.

Start with 303 million, end with 300.

One in a million high-school-age students attended the high school that had the combination of cash and foresight to buy a computer. Bill Gates happened to be one of them.

Gates is not shy about what this meant. "If there had been no Lakeside, there would have been no Microsoft," he told the school's graduating class in 2005.

Gates is staggeringly smart, even more hardworking, and as a teenager had a vision for computers that even most seasoned computer executives couldn't grasp. He also had a one in a million head start by going to school at Lakeside.

Now let me tell you about Gates' friend Kent Evans. He experienced an equally powerful dose of luck's close sibling, risk.

Bill Gates and Paul Allen became household names thanks to Microsoft's success. But back at Lakeside there was a third member of this gang of high-school computer prodigies.

Kent Evans and Bill Gates became best friends in eighth grade. Evans was, by Gates' own account, the best student in the class.

The two talked "on the phone ridiculous amounts," Gates recalls in the documentary *Inside Bill's Brain*. "I still know Kent's phone number," he says. "525-7851."

Evans was as skilled with computers as Gates and Allen. Lakeside once struggled to manually put together the school's class schedule—a maze of complexity to get hundreds of students the classes they need at times that don't conflict with other courses. The school tasked Bill and Kent—children, by any measure—to build a computer program to solve the problem. It worked.

And unlike Paul Allen, Kent shared Bill's business mind and endless ambition. "Kent always had the big briefcase, like a lawyer's briefcase," Gates recalls. "We were always scheming about what we'd be doing five or six years in the future. Should we go be CEOs? What kind of impact could you have? Should we go be generals? Should we go be ambassadors?" Whatever it was, Bill and Kent knew they'd do it together.

After reminiscing on his friendship with Kent, Gates trails off. "We would have kept working together. I'm sure we would have gone to college together." Kent could have been a founding partner of Microsoft with Gates and Allen.

But it would never happen. Kent died in a mountaineering accident before he graduated high school.

Every year there are around three dozen mountaineering deaths in the United States.[9] The odds of being killed on a mountain in high school are roughly one in a million.

Bill Gates experienced one in a million luck by ending up at

Lakeside. Kent Evans experienced one in a million risk by never getting to finish what he and Gates set out to achieve. The same force, the same magnitude, working in opposite directions.

Luck and risk are both the reality that every outcome in life is guided by forces other than individual effort. They are so similar that you can't believe in one without equally respecting the other. They both happen because the world is too complex to allow 100% of your actions to dictate 100% of your outcomes. They are driven by the same thing: You are one person in a game with seven billion other people and infinite moving parts. The accidental impact of actions outside of your control can be more consequential than the ones you consciously take.

But both are so hard to measure, and hard to accept, that they too often go overlooked. For every Bill Gates there is a Kent Evans who was just as skilled and driven but ended up on the other side of life roulette.

If you give luck and risk their proper respect, you realize that when judging people's financial success—both your own and others'—it's never as good or as bad as it seems.

Years ago I asked economist Robert Shiller, who won the Nobel Prize in economics, "What do you want to know about investing that we can't know?"

"The exact role of luck in successful outcomes," he answered.

I love that response, because no one actually thinks luck doesn't play a role in financial success. But since it's hard to quantify luck and rude to suggest people's success is owed to it, the default stance is often to implicitly ignore luck as a factor of success.

If I say, "There are a billion investors in the world. By sheer chance, would you expect 10 of them to become billionaires predominantly off luck?" You would reply, "Of course." But then if I ask you to name those investors—to their face—you will likely back down.

When judging others, attributing success to luck makes you look jealous and mean, even if we know it exists. And when judging yourself, attributing success to luck can be too demoralizing to accept.

Economist Bhashkar Mazumder has shown that incomes among brothers are more correlated than height or weight. If you are rich and tall, your brother is more likely to also be rich than he is tall. I think most of us intuitively know this is true—the quality of your education and the doors that open for you are heavily linked to your parents' socioeconomic status. But find me two rich brothers and I'll show you two men who do not think this study's findings apply to them.

Failure—which can be anything from bankruptcy to not meeting a personal goal—is equally abused.

Did failed businesses not try hard enough? Were bad investments not thought through well enough? Are wayward careers due to laziness? Sometimes, yes. Of course.

But how much? It's so hard to know. Everything worth pursuing has less than 100% odds of succeeding, and risk is just what happens when you end up on the unfortunate side of that equation. Just as with luck, the story gets too hard, too messy, too complex if we try to pick apart how much of an outcome was a conscious decision versus a risk.

Say I buy a stock, and five years later it's gone nowhere. It's possible that I made a bad decision by buying it in the first place. It's also possible that I made a good decision that had an 80% chance of making money, and I just happened to end up on the side of the unfortunate 20%. How do I know which is which? Did I make a mistake, or did I just experience the reality of risk?

It's possible to statistically measure whether some decisions were wise. But in the real world, day to day, we simply don't. It's too hard. We prefer simple stories, which are easy but often devilishly misleading.

After spending years around investors and business leaders I've come to realize that someone else's failure is usually attributed to bad decisions, while your own failures are usually chalked up to the dark side of risk. When judging your failures I'm likely to prefer a clean and simple story of cause and effect, because I don't know what's going on inside your head. "You had a bad outcome so it must have been caused by a bad decision" is the story that makes the most sense to me. But when judging myself I can make up a wild narrative justifying my past decisions and attributing bad outcomes to risk.

The cover of *Forbes* magazine does not celebrate poor investors who made good decisions but happened to experience the unfortunate side of risk. But it almost certainly celebrates rich investors who made OK or even reckless decisions and happened to get lucky. Both flipped the same coin that happened to land on a different side.

The dangerous part of this is that we're all trying to learn about what works and what doesn't with money.

What investing strategies work? Which ones don't?

What business strategies work? Which ones don't?

How do you get rich? How do you avoid being poor?

We tend to seek out these lessons by observing successes and failures and saying, "Do what she did, avoid what he did."

If we had a magic wand we would find out exactly what proportion of these outcomes were caused by actions that are repeatable, versus the role of random risk and luck that swayed those actions one way or the other. But we don't have a magic wand. We have brains that prefer easy answers without much appetite for nuance. So identifying the traits we should emulate or avoid can be agonizingly hard.

Let me tell you another story of someone who, like Bill Gates, was wildly successful, but whose success is hard to pin down as being caused by luck or skill.

Cornelius Vanderbilt had just finished a series of business deals to expand his railroad empire.

One of his business advisors leaned in to tell Vanderbilt that every transaction he agreed to broke the law.

"My God, John," said Vanderbilt, "You don't suppose you can run a railroad in accordance with the statutes of the State of New York, do you?"[10]

My first thought when reading this was: "That attitude is why he was so successful." Laws didn't accommodate railroads during Vanderbilt's day. So he said "to hell with it" and went ahead anyway.

Vanderbilt was wildly successful. So it's tempting to view his law-flaunting—which was notorious and vital to his success—as sage wisdom. That scrappy visionary let nothing get in his way!

But how dangerous is that analysis? No sane person would recommend flagrant crime as an entrepreneurial trait. You can easily imagine Vanderbilt's story turning out much different—an outlaw whose young company collapsed under court order.

So we have a problem here.

You can praise Vanderbilt for flaunting the law with as much passion as you criticize Enron for doing the same. Perhaps one got lucky by avoiding the arm of the law while the other found itself on the side of risk.

John D. Rockefeller is similar. His frequent circumventing of the law—a judge once called his company "no better than a common thief"—is often portrayed by historians as cunning business smarts. Maybe it was. But when does the narrative shift from, "You didn't let outdated laws get in the way of innovation," to "You committed a crime?" Or how little would the story have to shift for the narrative to have turned from "Rockefeller was a genius, try to learn from his successes," to "Rockefeller was a criminal, try to learn from his business failures." Very little.

"What do I care about the law?" Vanderbilt once said. "Ain't I got the power?"

He did, and it worked. But it's easy to imagine those being the last words of a story with a very different outcome. The line between bold and reckless can be thin. When we don't give risk and luck their proper billing it's often invisible.

Benjamin Graham is known as one of the greatest investors of all time, the father of value investing and the early mentor of Warren Buffett. But the majority of Benjamin Graham's investing success was due to owning an enormous chunk of GEICO stock which, by his own admission, broke nearly every diversification rule that Graham himself laid out in his famous texts. Where does the thin line between bold and reckless fall here? I don't know. Graham wrote about his GEICO bonanza: "One lucky break, or one supremely shrewd decision—can we tell them apart?" Not easily.

We similarly think Mark Zuckerberg is a genius for turning down Yahoo!'s 2006 $1 billion offer to buy his company. He saw the future and stuck to his guns. But people criticize Yahoo! with as much passion for turning down its own big buyout offer from Microsoft—those fools should have cashed out while they could! What is the lesson for entrepreneurs here? I have no idea, because risk and luck are so hard to pin down.

There are so many examples of this.

Countless fortunes (and failures) owe their outcome to leverage.

The best (and worst) managers drive their employees as hard as they can.

"The customer is always right" and "customers don't know what they want" are both accepted business wisdom.

The line between "inspiringly bold" and "foolishly reckless" can be a millimeter thick and only visible with hindsight.

Risk and luck are doppelgangers.

This is not an easy problem to solve. The difficulty in identifying what is luck, what is skill, and what is risk is one of the biggest problems we face when trying to learn about the best way to manage money.

But two things can point you in a better direction.

Be careful who you praise and admire. Be careful who you look down upon and wish to avoid becoming.

Or, just be careful when assuming that 100% of outcomes can be attributed to effort and decisions. After my son was born, I wrote him a letter that said, in part:

> Some people are born into families that encourage education; others are against it. Some are born into flourishing economies encouraging of entrepreneurship; others are born into war and destitution. I want you to be successful, and I want you to earn it. But realize that not all success is due to hard work, and not all poverty is due to laziness. Keep this in mind when judging people, including yourself.

Therefore, focus less on specific individuals and case studies and more on broad patterns.

Studying a specific person can be dangerous because we tend to study extreme examples—the billionaires, the CEOs, or the massive failures that dominate the news—and extreme examples are often the least applicable to other situations, given their complexity. The more extreme the outcome, the less likely you can apply its lessons to your own life, because the more likely the outcome was influenced by extreme ends of luck or risk.

You'll get closer to actionable takeaways by looking for broad patterns of success and failure. The more common the pattern, the more applicable it might be to your life. Trying to emulate Warren Buffett's investment success is hard, because his results are so extreme that the role of luck in his lifetime performance is very likely high, and luck isn't something you can reliably emulate. But realizing, as we'll see in chapter 7, that people who have control over their time tend to be happier in life is a broad and common enough observation that you can do something with it.

My favorite historian, Frederick Lewis Allen, spent his career depicting the life of the average, median American—how they lived, how they changed, what they did for work, what they ate for dinner, etc. There are more relevant lessons to take away from this kind of broad observation than there are in studying the extreme characters that tend to dominate the news.

Bill Gates once said, "Success is a lousy teacher. It seduces smart people into thinking they can't lose."

When things are going extremely well, realize it's not as good as you think. You are not invincible, and if you acknowledge that luck brought you success then you have to believe in luck's cousin, risk, which can turn your story around just as quickly.

But the same is true in the other direction.

Failure can be a lousy teacher, because it seduces smart people into thinking their decisions were terrible when sometimes they just reflect the unforgiving realities of risk. The trick when dealing with failure is arranging your financial life in a way that a bad investment here and a missed financial goal there won't wipe you out so you can keep playing until the odds fall in your favor.

But more important is that as much as we recognize the role of luck in success, the role of risk means we should forgive ourselves and leave room for understanding when judging failures.

Nothing is as good or as bad as it seems.

Now let's look at the stories of two men who pushed their luck.

3.

Never Enough

When rich people do crazy things.

JOHN BOGLE, THE Vanguard founder who passed away in 2019, once told a story about money that highlights something we don't think about enough:

> At a party given by a billionaire on Shelter Island, Kurt Vonnegut informs his pal, Joseph Heller, that their host, a hedge fund manager, had made more money in a single day than Heller had earned from his wildly popular novel *Catch-22* over its whole history. Heller responds, "Yes, but I have something he will never have … enough."
>
> *Enough.* I was stunned by the simple eloquence of that word—stunned for two reasons: first, because I have been given so much in my own life and, second, because Joseph Heller couldn't have been more accurate.
>
> For a critical element of our society, including many of the wealthiest and most powerful among us, there seems to be no limit today on what enough entails.

It's so smart, and so powerful.

Let me offer two examples of the dangers of not having enough, and what they can teach us.

Rajat Gupta was born in Kolkata and orphaned as a teenager. People talk about the privileged few who begin life on third base. Gupta couldn't even see the baseball stadium.

What he went on to achieve from those beginnings was simply phenomenal.

By his mid 40s Gupta was CEO of McKinsey, the world's most prestigious consulting firm. He retired in 2007 to take on roles with the United Nations and the World Economic Forum. He partnered on philanthropic work with Bill Gates. He sat on the board of directors of five public companies. From the slums of Kolkata, Gupta had quite literally become one of the most successful businessmen alive.

With his success came enormous wealth. By 2008 Gupta was reportedly worth $100 million.[11] It's an unfathomable sum of money to most. A five percent annual return on that much money generates almost $600 an hour, 24 hours a day.

He could have done anything he wanted in life.

And what he wanted, by all accounts, wasn't to be a mere centa-millionaire. Rajat Gupta wanted to be a billionaire. And he wanted it badly.

Gupta sat on the board of directors of Goldman Sachs, which surrounded him with some of the wealthiest investors in the world. One investor, citing the paydays of private equity tycoons, described Gupta like this: "I think he wants to be in that circle. That's a billionaire circle, right? Goldman is like the hundreds of millions circle, right?"[12]

Right. So Gupta found a lucrative side hustle.

In 2008, as Goldman Sachs stared at the wrath of the financial crisis, Warren Buffett planned to invest $5 billion into the bank to help it survive. As a Goldman board member Gupta learned of this transaction before the public. It was valuable information. Goldman's survival was in doubt and Buffett's backing would surely send its stock soaring.

Sixteen seconds after learning of the pending deal Gupta, who was dialed into the Goldman board meeting, hung up the phone and called a hedge fund manager named Raj Rajaratnam. The call wasn't recorded, but Rajaratnam immediately bought 175,000 shares of Goldman Sachs, so you can guess what was discussed. The Buffett-Goldman deal was announced to the public hours later. Goldman stock surged. Rajaratnam made a quick $1 million.

That was just one example of an alleged trend. The SEC claims Gupta's insider tips led to $17 million in profits.

It was easy money. And, for prosecutors, it was an even easier case.

Gupta and Rajaratnam both went to prison for insider trading, their careers and reputations irrevocably ruined.

Now consider Bernie Madoff. His crime is well known. Madoff is the most notorious Ponzi schemer since Charles Ponzi himself. Madoff swindled investors for two decades before his crime was revealed—ironically just weeks after Gupta's endeavor.

What's overlooked is that Madoff, like Gupta, was more than a fraudster. Before the Ponzi scheme that made Madoff famous he was a wildly successful and legitimate businessman.

Madoff was a market maker, a job that matches buyers and sellers of stocks. He was very good at it. Here's how *The Wall Street Journal* described Madoff's market-making firm in 1992:

> He has built a highly profitable securities firm, Bernard L. Madoff Investment Securities, which siphons a huge volume of stock trades away from the Big Board. The $740 million average daily volume of trades executed electronically by the Madoff firm off the exchange equals 9% of the New York exchange's. Mr. Madoff's firm can execute trades so quickly and cheaply that it actually pays other brokerage firms a penny a share to execute their customers' orders, profiting from the spread between bid and ask prices that most stocks trade for.

This is not a journalist inaccurately describing a fraud yet to be uncovered; Madoff's market-making business was legitimate. A former staffer said the market-making arm of Madoff's business made between $25 million and $50 million per year.

Bernie Madoff's legitimate, non-fraudulent business was by any measure a huge success. It made him hugely—and legitimately—wealthy.

And yet, the fraud.

The question we should ask of both Gupta and Madoff is why someone worth hundreds of millions of dollars would be so desperate for more money that they risked everything in pursuit of even more.

Crime committed by those living on the edge of survival is one thing. A Nigerian scam artist once told *The New York Times* that he felt guilty for hurting others, but "poverty will not make you feel the pain."[13]

What Gupta and Madoff did is something different. They already had everything: unimaginable wealth, prestige, power, freedom. And they threw it all away because they wanted more.

They had no sense of *enough*.

They are extreme examples. But there are non-criminal versions of this behavior.

The hedge fund Long-Term Capital Management was staffed with traders personally worth tens and hundreds of millions of dollars each, with most of their wealth invested in their own funds. Then they took so much risk in the quest for more that they managed to lose everything—in 1998, in the middle of the greatest bull market and strongest economy in history. Warren Buffett later put it:

> To make money they didn't have and didn't need, they risked what they did have and did need. And that's foolish. It is just plain foolish. If you risk something that is important to you for something that is unimportant to you, it just does not make any sense.

There is no reason to risk what you have and need for what you don't have and don't need.

It's one of those things that's as obvious as it is overlooked.

Few of us will ever have $100 million, as Gupta or Madoff did. But a measurable percentage of those reading this book will, at some point in their life, earn a salary or have a sum of money sufficient to cover every reasonable thing they need and a lot of what they want.

If you're one of them, remember a few things.

1. The hardest financial skill is getting the goalpost to stop moving.

But it's one of the most important. If expectations rise with results there is no logic in striving for more because you'll feel the same after putting in extra effort. It gets dangerous when the taste of having more—more money, more power, more prestige—increases ambition faster than satisfaction. In that case one step forward pushes the goalpost two steps ahead. You feel as if you're falling behind, and the only way to catch up is to take greater and greater amounts of risk.

Modern capitalism is a pro at two things: generating wealth and generating envy. Perhaps they go hand in hand; wanting to surpass your peers can be the fuel of hard work. But life isn't any fun without a sense of *enough*. Happiness, as it's said, is just results minus expectations.

2. Social comparison is the problem here.

Consider a rookie baseball player who earns $500,000 a year. He is, by any definition, rich. But say he plays on the same team as Mike Trout, who has a 12-year, $430 million contract. By comparison, the rookie is broke. But then think about Mike Trout. Thirty-six million dollars per year is an insane amount of money. But to make it on the list of the top-ten highest-paid hedge fund managers in 2018 you needed to earn at least $340 million in one year.[14] That's who people like Trout might compare their incomes to. And the hedge fund manager who makes $340 million per year compares himself to the top five hedge fund managers, who earned at least $770 million in 2018. Those top managers can look ahead to people like Warren Buffett, whose personal fortune increased by $3.5 billion in 2018. And someone like Buffett could look ahead to Jeff Bezos, whose net worth increased by $24 billion in 2018—a sum that equates to more per minute than the "rich" baseball player made in a full year.

The point is that the ceiling of social comparison is so high that virtually no one will ever hit it. Which means it's a battle that can never be won, or that the only way to win is to not fight to begin with—to accept that you might have enough, even if it's less than those around you.

A friend of mine makes an annual pilgrimage to Las Vegas. One year he asked a dealer: What games do you play, and what casinos do you play in? The dealer, stone-cold serious, replied: "The only way to win in a Las Vegas casino is to exit as soon as you enter."

That's exactly how the game of trying to keep up with other people's wealth works, too.

3. "Enough" is not too little.

The idea of having "enough" might look like conservatism, leaving opportunity and potential on the table.

I don't think that's right.

"Enough" is realizing that the opposite—an insatiable appetite for more—will push you to the point of regret.

The only way to know how much food you can eat is to eat until you're sick. Few try this because vomiting hurts more than any meal is good. For some reason the same logic doesn't translate to business and investing, and many will only stop reaching for more when they break and are forced to. This can be as innocent as burning out at work or a risky investment allocation you can't maintain. On the other end there's Rajat Guptas and Bernie Madoffs in the world, who resort to stealing because every dollar is worth reaching for regardless of consequence.

Whatever it is, the inability to deny a potential dollar will eventually catch up to you.

4. There are many things never worth risking, no matter the potential gain.

After he was released from prison Rajat Gupta told *The New York Times* he had learned a lesson:

> Don't get too attached to anything—your reputation, your accomplishments or any of it. I think about it now, what does it matter? O.K., this thing unjustly destroyed my reputation. That's only troubling if I am so attached to my reputation.

This seems like the worst possible takeaway from his experience, and what I imagine is the comforting self-justifications of a man who desperately wants his reputation back but knows it's gone.

Reputation is invaluable.

Freedom and independence are invaluable.

Family and friends are invaluable.

Being loved by those who you want to love you is invaluable.

Happiness is invaluable.

And your best shot at keeping these things is knowing when it's time to stop taking risks that might harm them. Knowing when you have *enough*.

The good news is that the most powerful tool for building *enough* is remarkably simple, and doesn't require taking risks that could damage any of these things. That's the next chapter.

4.

Confounding Compounding

$81.5 billion of Warren Buffett's $84.5 billion net worth came after his 65th birthday. Our minds are not built to handle such absurdities.

LESSONS FROM ONE field can often teach us something important about unrelated fields. Take the billion-year history of ice ages, and what they teach us about growing your money.

Our scientific knowledge of Earth is younger than you might think. Understanding how the world works often involves drilling deep below its surface, something we haven't been able to do until fairly recently. Isaac Newton calculated the movement of the stars hundreds of years before we understood some of the basics of our planet.

It was not until the 19th century that scientists agreed that Earth had, on multiple occasions, been covered in ice.[15] There was too much evidence to argue otherwise. All over the world sat fingerprints of a previously frozen world: huge boulders strewn in random locations; rock beds scraped down to thin layers. Evidence became clear that there had not been one ice age, but five distinct ones we could measure.

The amount of energy needed to freeze the planet, melt it anew, and freeze it over yet again is staggering. What on Earth (literally) could be causing these cycles? It must be the most powerful force on our planet.

And it was. Just not in the way anyone expected.

There were plenty of theories about why ice ages occurred. To account for their enormous geological influence the theories were equally grand. The uplifting of mountain ranges, it was thought, may have shifted the Earth's winds enough to alter the climate. Others favored the idea that ice was the natural state, interrupted by massive volcanic eruptions that warmed us up.

But none of these theories could account for the cycle of ice ages. The growth of mountain ranges or some massive volcano may explain one ice age. It could not explain the cyclical repetition of five.

In the early 1900s a Serbian scientist named Milutin Milanković studied the Earth's position relative to other planets and came up with the theory of ice ages that we now know is accurate: The gravitational pull of the sun and moon gently affect the Earth's motion and tilt toward the sun. During parts of this cycle—which can last tens of thousands of years—each of the Earth's hemispheres gets a little more, or a little less, solar radiation than they're used to.

And that is where the fun begins.

Milanković's theory initially assumed that a tilt of the Earth's hemispheres caused ravenous winters cold enough to turn the planet into ice. But a Russian meteorologist named Wladimir Köppen dug deeper into Milanković's work and discovered a fascinating nuance.

Moderately cool summers, not cold winters, were the icy culprit.

It begins when a summer never gets warm enough to melt the previous winter's snow. The leftover ice base makes it easier for snow to accumulate the following winter, which increases the odds of snow sticking around in the following summer, which attracts even more accumulation the following winter. Perpetual snow reflects more of the sun's rays, which exacerbates cooling, which brings more snowfall, and on and on. Within a few hundred years a seasonal snowpack grows into a continental ice sheet, and you're off to the races.

The same thing happens in reverse. An orbital tilt letting more sunlight in melts more of the winter snowpack, which reflects less light the following years, which increases temperatures, which prevents more snow the next year, and so on. That's the cycle.

The amazing thing here is how big something can grow from a relatively small change in conditions. You start with a thin layer of snow left over from a cool summer that no one would think anything of and then, in a geological blink of an eye, the entire Earth is covered in miles-thick ice. As glaciologist Gwen Schultz put it: "It is not necessarily the amount of snow that causes ice sheets but the fact that snow, however little, lasts."

The big takeaway from ice ages is that you don't need tremendous force to create tremendous results.

If something compounds—if a little growth serves as the fuel for future growth—a small starting base can lead to results so extraordinary they seem to defy logic. It can be so logic-defying that you underestimate what's possible, where growth comes from, and what it can lead to.

And so it is with money.

More than 2,000 books are dedicated to how Warren Buffett built his fortune. Many of them are wonderful. But few pay enough attention to the simplest fact: Buffett's fortune isn't due to just being a good investor, but being a good investor since he was literally a child.

As I write this Warren Buffett's net worth is $84.5 billion. Of that, $84.2 billion was accumulated after his 50th birthday. $81.5 billion came after he qualified for Social Security, in his mid-60s.

Warren Buffett is a phenomenal investor. But you miss a key point if you attach all of his success to investing acumen. The real key to his success is that he's been a phenomenal investor for three quarters of a century. Had he started investing in his 30s and retired in his 60s, few people would have ever heard of him.

Consider a little thought experiment.

Buffett began serious investing when he was 10 years old. By the time he was 30 he had a net worth of $1 million, or $9.3 million adjusted for inflation.[16]

What if he was a more normal person, spending his teens and 20s exploring the world and finding his passion, and by age 30 his net worth was, say, $25,000?

And let's say he still went on to earn the extraordinary annual investment returns he's been able to generate (22% annually), but quit investing and retired at age 60 to play golf and spend time with his grandkids.

What would a rough estimate of his net worth be today?

Not $84.5 billion.

$11.9 *million.*

99.9% less than his actual net worth.

Effectively all of Warren Buffett's financial success can be tied to the financial base he built in his pubescent years and the longevity he maintained in his geriatric years.

His skill is investing, but his secret is time.

That's how compounding works.

Think of this another way. Buffett is the richest investor of all time. But he's not actually the greatest—at least not when measured by average annual returns.

Jim Simons, head of the hedge fund Renaissance Technologies, has compounded money at 66% annually since 1988. No one comes close to this record. As we just saw, Buffett has compounded at roughly 22% annually, a third as much.

Simons' net worth, as I write, is $21 billion. He is—and I know how ridiculous this sounds given the numbers we're dealing with—75% less rich than Buffett.

Why the difference, if Simons is such a better investor? Because Simons did not find his investment stride until he was 50 years old. He's had less than half as many years to compound as Buffett. If

James Simons had earned his 66% annual returns for the 70-year span Buffett has built his wealth he would be worth—please hold your breath—sixty-three quintillion nine hundred quadrillion seven hundred eighty-one trillion seven hundred eighty billion seven hundred forty-eight million one hundred sixty thousand dollars.

These are ridiculous, impractical numbers. The point is that what seem like small changes in growth assumptions can lead to ridiculous, impractical numbers. And so when we are studying why something got to become as powerful as it has—why an ice age formed, or why Warren Buffett is so rich—we often overlook the key drivers of success.

I have heard many people say the first time they saw a compound interest table—or one of those stories about how much more you'd have for retirement if you began saving in your 20s versus your 30s—changed their life. But it probably didn't. What it likely did was *surprise* them, because the results intuitively didn't seem right. Linear thinking is so much more intuitive than exponential thinking. If I ask you to calculate 8+8+8+8+8+8+8+8+8 in your head, you can do it in a few seconds (it's 72). If I ask you to calculate 8×8×8×8×8×8×8×8×8, your head will explode (it's 134,217,728).

IBM made a 3.5 megabyte hard drive in the 1950s. By the 1960s things were moving into a few dozen megabytes. By the 1970s, IBM's Winchester drive held 70 megabytes. Then drives got exponentially smaller in size with more storage. A typical PC in the early 1990s held 200–500 megabytes.

And then … *wham*. Things exploded.

1999—Apple's iMac comes with a 6 gigabyte hard drive.

2003—120 gigs on the Power Mac.

2006—250 gigs on the new iMac.

2011—first 4 terabyte hard drive.

2017—60 terabyte hard drives.

2019—100 terabyte hard drives.

Put that all together: From 1950 to 1990 we gained 296 megabytes. From 1990 through today we gained 100 million megabytes.

If you were a technology optimist in the 1950s you may have predicted that practical storage would become 1,000 times larger. Maybe 10,000 times larger, if you were swinging for the fences. Few would have said "30 million times larger within my lifetime." But that's what happened.

The counterintuitive nature of compounding leads even the smartest of us to overlook its power. In 2004 Bill Gates criticized the new Gmail, wondering why anyone would need a gigabyte of storage. Author Steven Levy wrote, "Despite his currency with cutting-edge technologies, his mentality was anchored in the old paradigm of storage being a commodity that must be conserved." You never get accustomed to how quickly things can grow.

The danger here is that when compounding isn't intuitive we often ignore its potential and focus on solving problems through other means. Not because we're overthinking, but because we rarely stop to consider compounding potential.

None of the 2,000 books picking apart Buffett's success are titled *This Guy Has Been Investing Consistently for Three-Quarters of a Century.* But we know that's the key to the majority of his success. It's just hard to wrap your head around that math because it's not intuitive.

There are books on economic cycles, trading strategies, and sector bets. But the most powerful and important book should be called *Shut Up And Wait.* It's just one page with a long-term chart of economic growth.

The practical takeaway is that the counterintuitiveness of compounding may be responsible for the majority of disappointing trades, bad strategies, and successful investing attempts.

You can't blame people for devoting all their effort—effort in what they learn and what they do—to trying to earn the highest investment returns. It intuitively seems like the best way to get rich.

But good investing isn't necessarily about earning the highest returns, because the highest returns tend to be one-off hits that can't be repeated. It's about earning pretty good returns that you can stick with and which can be repeated for the longest period of time. That's when compounding runs wild.

The opposite of this—earning huge returns that can't be held onto—leads to some tragic stories. We'll need the next chapter to tell them.

5.

Getting Wealthy vs. Staying Wealthy

Good investing is not necessarily about making good decisions. It's about consistently not screwing up.

THERE ARE A million ways to get wealthy, and plenty of books on how to do so.

But there's only one way to stay wealthy: some combination of frugality and paranoia.

And that's a topic we don't discuss enough.

Let's begin with a quick story about two investors, neither of whom knew the other, but whose paths crossed in an interesting way almost a century ago.

Jesse Livermore was the greatest stock market trader of his day. Born in 1877, he became a professional trader before most people knew you could do such a thing. By age 30 he was worth the inflation-adjusted equivalent of $100 million.

By 1929 Jesse Livermore was already one of the most well-known investors in the world. The stock market crash that year that ushered in the Great Depression cemented his legacy in history.

More than a third of the stock market's value was wiped out in an October 1929 week whose days were later named Black Monday, Black Tuesday, and Black Thursday.

Livermore's wife Dorothy feared the worst when her husband returned home on October 29th. Reports of Wall Street speculators committing suicide were spreading across New York. She and her children greeted Jesse at the door in tears, while her mother was so distraught she hid in another room, screaming.

Jesse, according to biographer Tom Rubython, stood confused for a few moments before realizing what was happening.

He then broke the news to his family: In a stroke of genius and luck, he had been short the market, betting stocks would decline.

"You mean we are not ruined?" Dorothy asked.

"No darling, I have just had my best ever trading day—we are fabulously rich and can do whatever we like," Jesse said.

Dorothy ran to her mother and told her to be quiet.

In one day Jesse Livermore made the equivalent of more than $3 billion.

During one of the worst months in the history of the stock market he became one of the richest men in the world.

As Livermore's family celebrated their unfathomable success, another man wandered the streets of New York in desperation.

Abraham Germansky was a multimillionaire real estate developer who made a fortune during the roaring 1920s. As the economy boomed, he did what virtually every other successful New Yorker did in the late 1920s: bet heavily on the surging stock market.

On October 26th, 1929, *The New York Times* published an article that in two paragraphs portrays a tragic ending:

> Bernard H. Sandler, attorney of 225 Broadway, was asked yesterday morning by Mrs. Abraham Germansky of Mount Vernon to help find her husband, missing since Thursday Morning. Germansky, who is 50 years old and an east side real estate operator, was said by Sandler to have invested heavily in stocks.
>
> Sandler said he was told by Mrs. Germansky that a friend saw her husband late Thursday on Wall Street near the stock exchange. According to her informant, her husband was tearing a strip of ticker tape into bits and scattering it on the sidewalk as he walked toward Broadway.

And that, as far as we know, was the end of Abraham Germansky.

Here we have a contrast.

The October 1929 crash made Jesse Livermore one of the richest men in the world. It ruined Abraham Germansky, perhaps taking his life.

But fast-forward four years and the stories cross paths again.

After his 1929 blowout Livermore, overflowing with confidence, made larger and larger bets. He wound up far over his head, in increasing amounts of debt, and eventually lost everything in the stock market.

Broke and ashamed, he disappeared for two days in 1933. His wife set out to find him. "Jesse L. Livermore, the stock market operator, of 1100 Park Avenue missing and has not been seen since 3pm yesterday," *The New York Times* wrote in 1933.

He returned, but his path was set. Livermore eventually took his own life.

The timing was different, but Germansky and Livermore shared a character trait: They were both very good at getting wealthy, and equally bad at *staying* wealthy.

Even if "wealthy" is not a word you'd apply to yourself, the lessons from that observation apply to everyone, at all income levels.

Getting money is one thing.

Keeping it is another.

If I had to summarize money success in a single word it would be "survival."

As we'll see in chapter 6, 40% of companies successful enough to become publicly traded lost effectively all of their value over time. The Forbes 400 list of richest Americans has, on average, roughly 20% turnover per decade for causes that don't have to do with death or transferring money to another family member.[17]

Capitalism is hard. But part of the reason this happens is because getting money and keeping money are two different skills.

Getting money requires taking risks, being optimistic, and putting yourself out there.

But keeping money requires the opposite of taking risk. It requires humility, and fear that what you've made can be taken away from you just as fast. It requires frugality and an acceptance that at least some of what you've made is attributable to luck, so past success can't be relied upon to repeat indefinitely.

Michael Moritz, the billionaire head of Sequoia Capital, was asked by Charlie Rose why Sequoia was so successful. Moritz mentioned longevity, noting that some VC firms succeed for five or ten years, but Sequoia has prospered for four decades. Rose asked why that was:

> Moritz: I think we've always been afraid of going out of business.
>
> Rose: Really? So it's fear? Only the paranoid survive?
>
> Moritz: There's a lot of truth to that ... We assume that tomorrow won't be like yesterday. We can't afford to rest on our laurels. We can't be complacent. We can't assume that yesterday's success translates into tomorrow's good fortune.

Here again, survival.

Not "growth" or "brains" or "insight." The ability to stick around for a long time, without wiping out or being forced to give up, is what makes the biggest difference. This should be the cornerstone of your strategy, whether it's in investing or your career or a business you own.

There are two reasons why a survival mentality is so key with money.

One is the obvious: few gains are so great that they're worth wiping yourself out over.

The other, as we saw in chapter 4, is the counterintuitive math of compounding.

Compounding only works if you can give an asset years and years to grow. It's like planting oak trees: A year of growth will never show much progress, 10 years can make a meaningful difference, and 50 years can create something absolutely extraordinary.

But getting and keeping that extraordinary growth requires surviving all the unpredictable ups and downs that everyone inevitably experiences over time.

We can spend years trying to figure out how Buffett achieved his investment returns: how he found the best companies, the cheapest stocks, the best managers. That's hard. Less hard but equally important is pointing out what he didn't do.

He didn't get carried away with debt.

He didn't panic and sell during the 14 recessions he's lived through.

He didn't sully his business reputation.

He didn't attach himself to one strategy, one world view, or one passing trend.

He didn't rely on others' money (managing investments through a public company meant investors couldn't withdraw their capital).

He didn't burn himself out and quit or retire.

He survived. Survival gave him longevity. And longevity—investing consistently from age 10 to at least age 89—is what made compounding work wonders. That single point is what matters most when describing his success.

To show you what I mean, you have to hear the story of Rick Guerin.

You've likely heard of the investing duo of Warren Buffett and Charlie Munger. But 40 years ago there was a third member of the group, Rick Guerin.

Warren, Charlie, and Rick made investments together and

interviewed business managers together. Then Rick kind of disappeared, at least relative to Buffett and Munger's success. Investor Mohnish Pabrai once asked Buffett what happened to Rick. Mohnish recalled:

> [Warren said] "Charlie and I always knew that we would become incredibly wealthy. We were not in a hurry to get wealthy; we knew it would happen. Rick was just as smart as us, but he was in a hurry."
>
> What happened was that in the 1973–1974 downturn, Rick was levered with margin loans. And the stock market went down almost 70% in those two years, so he got margin calls. He sold his Berkshire stock to Warren—Warren actually said "I bought Rick's Berkshire stock"—at under $40 a piece. Rick was forced to sell because he was levered.[18]

Charlie, Warren, and Rick were equally skilled at getting wealthy. But Warren and Charlie had the added skill of staying wealthy. Which, over time, is the skill that matters most.

Nassim Taleb put it this way: "Having an 'edge' and surviving are two different things: the first requires the second. You need to avoid ruin. At all costs."

Applying the survival mindset to the real world comes down to appreciating three things.

1. More than I want big returns, I want to be financially unbreakable. And if I'm unbreakable I actually think I'll get the biggest returns, because I'll be able to stick around long enough for compounding to work wonders.

No one wants to hold cash during a bull market. They want to own assets that go up a lot. You look and feel conservative holding cash during a bull market, because you become acutely aware of how much return you're giving up by not owning the good stuff. Say cash earns 1% and stocks return 10% a year. That 9% gap will gnaw at you every day.

But if that cash prevents you from having to sell your stocks during a bear market, the actual return you earned on that cash is not 1% a year—it could be many multiples of that, because preventing one desperate, ill-timed stock sale can do more for your lifetime returns than picking dozens of big-time winners.

Compounding doesn't rely on earning big returns. Merely good returns sustained uninterrupted for the longest period of time—especially in times of chaos and havoc—will always win.

2. Planning is important, but the most important part of every plan is to plan on the plan not going according to plan.

What's the saying? You plan, God laughs. Financial and investment planning are critical, because they let you know whether your current actions are within the realm of reasonable. But few plans of any kind survive their first encounter with the real world. If you're projecting your income, savings rate, and market returns over the next 20 years, think about all the big stuff that's happened in the last 20 years that no one could have foreseen: September 11th, a housing boom and bust that caused nearly 10 million Americans to lose their homes, a financial crisis that caused almost nine million to lose their jobs, a record-breaking stock-market rally that ensued, and a coronavirus that shakes the world as I write this.

A plan is only useful if it can survive reality. And a future filled with unknowns is everyone's reality.

A good plan doesn't pretend this weren't true; it embraces it and emphasizes room for error. The more you need specific elements of a plan to be true, the more fragile your financial life becomes. If there's enough room for error in your savings rate that you can say, "It'd be great if the market returns 8% a year over the next 30 years, but if it only does 4% a year I'll still be OK," the more valuable your plan becomes.

Many bets fail not because they were wrong, but because they were mostly right in a situation that required things to be exactly right. Room for error—often called margin of safety—is one of the most underappreciated forces in finance. It comes in many forms: A frugal budget, flexible thinking, and a loose timeline—anything that lets you live happily with a range of outcomes.

It's different from being conservative. Conservative is avoiding a certain level of risk. Margin of safety is raising the odds of success at a given level of risk by increasing your chances of survival. Its magic is that the higher your margin of safety, the smaller your edge needs to be to have a favorable outcome.

3. A barbelled personality—optimistic about the future, but paranoid about what will prevent you from getting to the future—is vital.

Optimism is usually defined as a belief that things will go well. But that's incomplete. Sensible optimism is a belief that the odds are in your favor, and over time things will balance out to a good outcome even if what happens in between is filled with misery. And in fact you *know* it will be filled with misery. You can be optimistic that the long-term growth trajectory is up and to the right, but equally sure that the road between now and then is filled with landmines, and always will be. Those two things are not mutually exclusive.

The idea that something can gain over the long run while being a basketcase in the short run is not intuitive, but it's how a lot of things work in life. By age 20 the average person can lose roughly half the synaptic connections they had in their brain at age two, as inefficient and redundant neural pathways are cleared out. But the average 20-year-old is much smarter than the average two-year-old. Destruction in the face of progress is not only possible, but an efficient way to get rid of excess.

Imagine if you were a parent and could see inside your child's brain. Every morning you notice fewer synaptic connections in your kid's head. You would panic! You would say, "This can't be right, there's loss and destruction here. We need an intervention. We need to see a doctor!" But you don't. What you are witnessing is the normal path of progress.

Economies, markets, and careers often follow a similar path—growth amid loss.

Here's how the U.S. economy performed over the last 170 years:

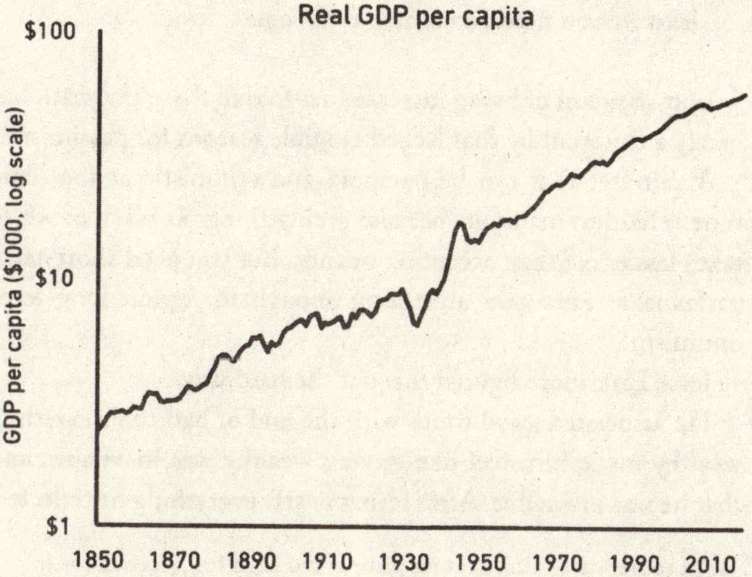

But do you know what happened during this period? Where do we begin ...

- 1.3 million Americans died while fighting nine major wars.
- Roughly 99.9% of all companies that were created went out of business.
- Four U.S. presidents were assassinated.
- 675,000 Americans died in a single year from a flu pandemic.
- 30 separate natural disasters killed at least 400 Americans each.
- 33 recessions lasted a cumulative 48 years.
- The number of forecasters who predicted any of those recessions rounds to zero.
- The stock market fell more than 10% from a recent high at least 102 times.
- Stocks lost a third of their value at least 12 times.
- Annual inflation exceeded 7% in 20 separate years.
- The words "economic pessimism" appeared in newspapers at least 29,000 times, according to Google.

Our standard of living increased 20-fold in these 170 years, but barely a day went by that lacked tangible reasons for pessimism.

A mindset that can be paranoid and optimistic at the same time is hard to maintain, because seeing things as black or white takes less effort than accepting nuance. But you need short-term paranoia to keep you alive long enough to exploit long-term optimism.

Jesse Livermore figured this out the hard way.

He associated good times with the end of bad times. Getting wealthy made him feel like staying wealthy was inevitable, and that he was invincible. After losing nearly everything he reflected:

> I sometimes think that no price is too high for a speculator to pay to learn that which will keep him from getting the swelled head. A great many smashes by brilliant men can be traced directly to the swelled head.

"It's an expensive disease," he said, "everywhere to everybody."

Next, we'll look at another way growth in the face of adversity can be so hard to wrap your head around.

6.

Tails, You Win

You can be wrong half the time and still make a fortune.

"I've been banging away at this thing for 30 years. I think the simple math is, some projects work and some don't. There's no reason to belabor either one. Just get on to the next."

—Brad Pitt accepting a Screen Actors Guild Award

HEINZ BERGGRUEN FLED Nazi Germany in 1936. He settled in America, where he studied literature at U.C. Berkeley.

By most accounts he did not show particular promise in his youth. But by the 1990s Berggruen was, by any measure, one of the most successful art dealers of all time.

In 2000 Berggruen sold part of his massive collection of Picassos, Braques, Klees, and Matisses to the German government for more than 100 million euros. It was such a bargain that the Germans effectively considered it a donation. The private market value of the collection was well over a $1 billion.

That one person can collect huge quantities of masterpieces is astounding. Art is as subjective as it gets. How could anyone have foreseen, early in life, what were to become the most sought-after works of the century?

You could say "skill."

You could say "luck."

The investment firm Horizon Research has a third explanation. And it's very relevant to investors.

"The great investors bought vast quantities of art," the firm writes.[19] "A subset of the collections turned out to be great investments, and they were held for a sufficiently long period of time to allow the portfolio return to converge upon the return of the best elements in the portfolio. That's all that happens."

The great art dealers operated like index funds. They bought everything they could. And they bought it in portfolios, not individual pieces they happened to like. Then they sat and waited for a few winners to emerge.

That's all that happens.

Perhaps 99% of the works someone like Berggruen acquired in his life turned out to be of little value. But that doesn't particularly matter if the other 1% turn out to be the work of someone like Picasso. Berggruen could be wrong most of the time and still end up stupendously right.

A lot of things in business and investing work this way. Long tails—the farthest ends of a distribution of outcomes—have tremendous influence in finance, where a small number of events can account for the majority of outcomes.

That can be hard to deal with, even if you understand the math. It is not intuitive that an investor can be wrong half the time and still make a fortune. It means we underestimate how normal it is for a lot of things to fail. Which causes us to overreact when they do.

Steamboat Willie put Walt Disney on the map as an animator. Business success was another story. Disney's first studio went bankrupt. His films were monstrously expensive to produce, and financed at outrageous terms. By the mid-1930s Disney had produced more than 400 cartoons. Most of them were short, most of them were beloved by viewers, and most of them lost a fortune.

Snow White and the Seven Dwarfs changed everything.

The $8 million it earned in the first six months of 1938 was an order of magnitude higher than anything the company earned previously.

It transformed Disney Studios. All company debts were paid off. Key employees got retention bonuses. The company purchased a new state-of-the-art studio in Burbank, where it remains today. An Oscar turned Walt from famous to full-blown celebrity. By 1938 he had produced several hundred hours of film. But in business terms, the 83 minutes of *Snow White* were all that mattered.

Anything that is huge, profitable, famous, or influential is the result of a tail event—an outlying one-in-thousands or millions event. And most of our attention goes to things that are huge, profitable, famous, or influential. When most of what we pay attention to is the result of a tail, it's easy to underestimate how rare and powerful they are.

Some tail-driven industries are obvious. Take venture capital. If a VC makes 50 investments they likely expect half of them to fail, 10 to do pretty well, and one or two to be bonanzas that drive 100% of the fund's returns. Investment firm Correlation Ventures once crunched the numbers.[20] Out of more than 21,000 venture financings from 2004 to 2014:

65% lost money.

Two and a half percent of investments made 10x–20x.

One percent made more than a 20x return.

Half a percent—about 100 companies out of 21,000—earned 50x or more. That's where the majority of the industry's returns come from.

This, you might think, is what makes venture capital so risky. And everyone investing in VC knows it's risky. Most startups fail and the world is only kind enough to allow a few mega successes.

If you want safer, predictable, and more stable returns, you invest in large public companies.

Or so you might think.

Remember, tails drive *everything*.

The distribution of success among large public stocks over time is not much different than it is in venture capital.

Most public companies are duds, a few do well, and a handful become extraordinary winners that account for the majority of the stock market's returns.

J.P. Morgan Asset Management once published the distribution of returns for the Russell 3000 Index—a big, broad, collection of public companies—since 1980.[21]

Forty percent of all Russell 3000 stock components lost at least 70% of their value and never recovered over this period.

Effectively all of the index's overall returns came from 7% of component companies that outperformed by at least two standard deviations.

That's the kind of thing you'd expect from venture capital. But it's what happened inside a boring, diversified index.

This thumping of most public companies spares no industry. More than half of all public technology and telecom companies lose most of their value and never recover. Even among public utilities the failure rate is more than 1 in 10:

Percentage of companies experiencing "catastrophic loss," 1980–2014

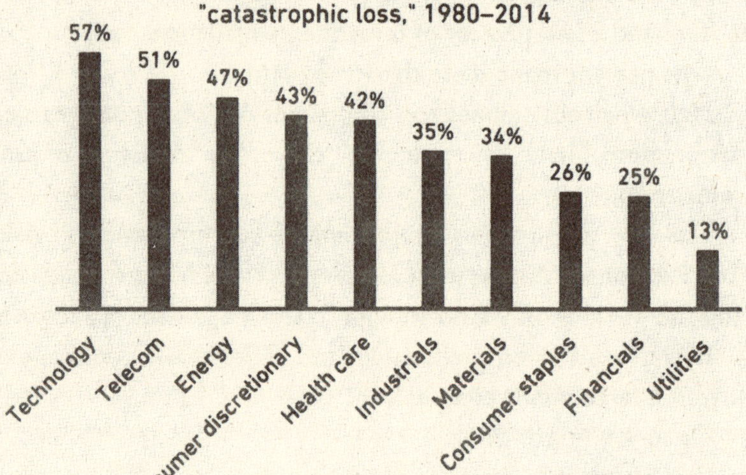

The interesting thing here is that you have to have achieved a certain level of success to become a public company and a member of the Russell 3000. These are established corporations, not fly-by-night startups. Even still, most have lifespans measured in years, not generations.

Take an example one of these companies: Carolco, a former member of the Russell 3000 Index.

It produced some of the biggest films of the 1980s and 1990s, including the first three Rambo films, *Terminator 2*, *Basic Instinct*, and *Total Recall*.

Carolco went public in 1987. It was a huge success, churning out hit after hit. It did half a billion dollars in revenue in 1991, commanding a market cap of $400 million—big money back then, especially for a film studio.

And then it failed.

The blockbusters stopped, a few big-budget projects flopped, and by the mid-1990s Carolco was history. It went bankrupt in 1996. Stock goes to zero, have a nice day. A catastrophic loss. And one that 4 in 10 public companies experience over time. Carolco's story is not worth telling because it's unique, but because it's common.

Here's the most important part of this story: The Russell 3000 has increased more than 73-fold since 1980. That is a spectacular return. That is *success*.

Forty percent of the companies in the index were effectively failures. But the 7% of components that performed extremely well were more than enough to offset the duds. Just like Heinz Berggruen, but with Microsoft and Walmart instead of Picasso and Matisse.

Not only do a few companies account for most of the market's return, but within those companies are even more tail events.

In 2018, Amazon drove 6% of the S&P 500's returns. And Amazon's growth is almost entirely due to Prime and Amazon Web Services, which itself are tail events in a company that has experimented with hundreds of products, from the Fire Phone to travel agencies.

Apple was responsible for almost 7% of the index's returns in 2018. And it is driven overwhelmingly by the iPhone, which in the world of tech products is as tail-y as tails get.

And who's working at these companies? Google's hiring acceptance rate is 0.2%.[22] Facebook's is 0.1%.[23] Apple's is about 2%.[24] So the people working on these tail projects that drive tail returns have tail careers.

The idea that a few things account for most results is not just true for companies in your investment portfolio. It's also an important part of your own behavior as an investor.

Napoleon's definition of a military genius was, "The man who can do the average thing when all those around him are going crazy."

It's the same in investing.

Most financial advice is about *today*. What should you do *right now*, and what stocks look like good buys *today*?

But most of the time *today* is not that important. Over the course of your lifetime as an investor the decisions that you make today or tomorrow or next week will not matter nearly as much as what you do during the small number of days—likely 1% of the time or less—when everyone else around you is going crazy.

Consider what would happen if you saved $1 every month from 1900 to 2019.

You could invest that $1 into the U.S. stock market every month, rain or shine. It doesn't matter if economists are screaming about a looming recession or new bear market. You just keep investing. Let's call an investor who does this Sue.

But maybe investing during a recession is too scary. So perhaps you invest your $1 in the stock market when the economy is not in a recession, sell everything when it's in a recession and save your monthly dollar in cash, and invest everything back into the stock market when the recession ends. We'll call this investor Jim.

Or perhaps it takes a few months for a recession to scare you out, and then it takes a while to regain confidence before you get back in the market. You invest $1 in stocks when there's no recession, sell six months after a recession begins, and invest back in six months after a recession ends. We'll call you Tom.

How much money would these three investors end up with over time?

Sue ends up with $435,551.

Jim has $257,386.

Tom $234,476.

Sue wins by a mile.

There were 1,428 months between 1900 and 2019. Just over 300 of them were during a recession. So by keeping her cool during just the 22% of the time the economy was in or near a recession, Sue ends up with almost three-quarters more money than Jim or Tom.

To give a more recent example: How you behaved as an investor during a few months in late 2008 and early 2009 will likely have more impact on your lifetime returns than everything you did from 2000 to 2008.

There is the old pilot quip that their jobs are "hours and hours of boredom punctuated by moments of sheer terror." It's the same in investing. Your success as an investor will be determined by how you respond to punctuated moments of terror, not the years spent on cruise control.

A good definition of an investing genius is the man or woman who can do the average thing when all those around them are going crazy.

Tails drive everything.

When you accept that tails drive everything in business, investing, and finance you realize that it's normal for lots of things to go wrong, break, fail, and fall.

If you're a good stock picker you'll be right maybe half the time.

If you're a good business leader maybe half of your product and strategy ideas will work.

If you're a good investor most years will be just OK, and plenty will be bad.

If you're a good worker you'll find the right company in the right field after several attempts and trials.

And that's if you're good.

Peter Lynch is one of the best investors of our time. "If you're terrific in this business, you're right six times out of 10," he once said.

There are fields where you must be perfect every time. Flying a plane, for example. Then there are fields where you want to be at least pretty good nearly all the time. A restaurant chef, let's say.

Investing, business, and finance are just not like these fields.

Something I've learned from both investors and entrepreneurs is that no one makes good decisions all the time. The most impressive people are packed full of horrendous ideas that are often acted upon.

Take Amazon. It's not intuitive to think a failed product launch at a major company would be normal and fine. Intuitively, you'd think the CEO should apologize to shareholders. But CEO Jeff Bezos said shortly after the disastrous launch of the company's Fire Phone:

> If you think that's a big failure, we're working on much bigger failures right now. I am not kidding. Some of them are going to make the Fire Phone look like a tiny little blip.

It's OK for Amazon to lose a lot of money on the Fire Phone because it will be offset by something like Amazon Web Services that earns tens of billions of dollars. Tails to the rescue.

Netflix CEO Reed Hastings once announced his company was canceling several big-budget productions. He responded:

> Our hit ratio is way too high right now. I'm always pushing the content team. We have to take more risk. You have to try more crazy things, because we should have a higher cancel rate overall.

These are not delusions or failures of responsibility. They are a smart acknowledgement of how tails drive success. For every Amazon Prime or *Orange is The New Black* you know, with certainty, that you'll have some duds.

Part of why this isn't intuitive is because in most fields we only see the finished product, not the losses incurred that led to the tail-success product.

The Chris Rock I see on TV is hilarious, flawless. The Chris Rock that performs in dozens of small clubs each year is just OK. That is by design. No comedic genius is smart enough to preemptively know what jokes will land well. Every big comedian tests their material in small clubs before using it in big venues. Rock was once asked if he missed small clubs. He responded:

> When I start a tour, it's not like I start out in arenas. Before this last tour I performed in this place in New Brunswick called the Stress Factory. I did about 40 or 50 shows getting ready for the tour.

One newspaper profiled these small-club sessions. It described Rock thumbing through pages of notes and fumbling with material. "I'm going to have to cut some of these jokes," he says mid-skit. The good jokes I see on Netflix are the tails that stuck out of a universe of hundreds of attempts.

A similar thing happens in investing. It's easy to find Warren Buffett's net worth, or his average annual returns. Or even his best, most notable investments. They're right there in the open, and they're what people talk about.

It's much harder to piece together every investment he's made over his career. No one talks about the dud picks, the ugly businesses, the poor acquisitions. But they're a big part of Buffett's story. They are the other side of tail-driven returns.

At the Berkshire Hathaway shareholder meeting in 2013 Warren Buffett said he's owned 400 to 500 stocks during his life and made most of his money on 10 of them. Charlie Munger followed up: "If you remove just a few of Berkshire's top investments, its long-term track record is pretty average."

When we pay special attention to a role model's successes we overlook that their gains came from a small percent of their actions. That makes our own failures, losses, and setbacks feel like we're doing something wrong. But it's possible we are wrong, or just sort of right, just as often as the masters are. They may have been *more right* when they were right, but they could have been wrong just as often as you.

"It's not whether you're right or wrong that's important," George Soros once said, "but how much money you make when you're right and how much you lose when you're wrong." You can be wrong half the time and still make a fortune.

There are 100 billion planets in our galaxy and only one, as far as we know, with intelligent life.

The fact that you are reading this book is the result of the longest tail you can imagine.

That's something to be happy about. Next, let's look at how money can make you even happier.

7.

Freedom

Controlling your time is the highest dividend money pays.

THE HIGHEST FORM of wealth is the ability to wake up every morning and say, "I can do whatever I want today."

People want to become wealthier to make them happier. Happiness is a complicated subject because everyone's different. But if there's a common denominator in happiness—a universal fuel of joy—it's that people want to control their lives.

The ability to do what you want, when you want, with who you want, for as long as you want, is priceless. It is the highest dividend money pays.

Angus Campbell was a psychologist at the University of Michigan. Born in 1910, his research took place during an age when psychology was overwhelmingly focused on disorders that brought people down—things like depression, anxiety, schizophrenia.

Campbell wanted to know what made people happy. His 1981 book, *The Sense of Wellbeing in America*, starts by pointing out that people are generally happier than many psychologists assumed. But some were clearly doing better than others. And you couldn't necessarily group them by income, or geography, or education, because so many in each of those categories end up chronically unhappy.

The most powerful common denominator of happiness was simple. Campbell summed it up:

> Having a strong sense of controlling one's life is a more dependable predictor of positive feelings of wellbeing than any of the objective conditions of life we have considered.

More than your salary. More than the size of your house. More than the prestige of your job. Control over doing what you want, when you want to, with the people you want to, is the broadest lifestyle variable that makes people happy.

Money's greatest intrinsic value—and this can't be overstated—is its ability to give you control over your time. To obtain, bit by bit, a level of independence and autonomy that comes from unspent assets that give you greater control over what you can do and when you can do it.

A small amount of wealth means the ability to take a few days off work when you're sick without breaking the bank. Gaining that ability is huge if you don't have it.

A bit more means waiting for a good job to come around after you get laid off, rather than having to take the first one you find. That can be life changing.

Six months' emergency expenses means not being terrified of your boss, because you know you won't be ruined if you have to take some time off to find a new job.

More still means the ability to take a job with lower pay but flexible hours. Maybe one with a shorter commute. Or being able to deal with a medical emergency without the added burden of worrying about how you'll pay for it.

Then there's retiring when you want to, instead of when you need to.

Using your money to buy time and options has a lifestyle benefit few luxury goods can compete with.

Throughout college I wanted to be an investment banker. There was only one reason why: they made a lot of money. That was the only drive, and one I was 100% positive would make me happier once I got it. I scored a summer internship at an investment bank in Los Angeles in my junior year, and thought I won the career lottery. This is all I ever wanted.

On my first day I realized why investment bankers make a lot of money: They work longer and more controlled hours than I knew humans could handle. Actually, most can't handle it. Going home before midnight was considered a luxury, and there was a saying in the office: "If you don't come to work on Saturday, don't bother coming back on Sunday." The job was intellectually stimulating, paid well, and made me feel important. But every waking second of my time became a slave to my boss's demands, which was enough to turn it into one of the most miserable experiences of my life. It was a four-month internship. I lasted a month.

The hardest thing about this was that I loved the work. And I wanted to work hard. But doing something you love on a schedule you can't control can feel the same as doing something you hate.

There is a name for this feeling. Psychologists call it reactance. Jonah Berger, a marketing professor at the University of Pennsylvania, summed it up well:

> People like to feel like they're in control—in the drivers' seat. When we try to get them to do something, they feel disempowered. Rather than feeling like they made the choice, they feel like we made it for them. So they say no or do something else, even when they might have originally been happy to go along.[25]

When you accept how true that statement is, you realize that aligning money towards a life that lets you do what you want, when you want, with who you want, where you want, for as long as you want, has incredible return.

Derek Sivers, a successful entrepreneur, once wrote about a friend who asked him to tell the story about how he got rich:

> I had a day job in midtown Manhattan paying $20K per year—about minimum wage ... I never ate out, and never took a taxi.

My cost of living was about $1000/month, and I was earning $1800/month. I did this for two years, and saved up $12,000. I was 22 years old.

Once I had $12,000 I could quit my job and become a full-time musician. I knew I could get a few gigs per month to pay my cost of living. So I was free. I quit my job a month later, and never had a job again.

When I finished telling my friend this story, he asked for more. I said no, that was it. He said, "No, what about when you sold your company?"

I said no, that didn't make a big difference in my life. That was just more money in the bank. The difference happened when I was 22.[26]

The United States is the richest nation in the history of the world. But there is little evidence that its citizens are, on average, happier today than they were in the 1950s, when wealth and income were much lower—even at the median level and adjusted for inflation. A 2019 Gallup poll of 150,000 people in 140 countries found that about 45% of Americans said they felt "a lot of worry" the previous day.[27] The global average was 39%. Fifty-five percent of Americans said they felt "a lot of stress" the previous day. For the rest of the world, 35% said the same.

Part of what's happened here is that we've used our greater wealth to buy bigger and better stuff. But we've simultaneously given up more control over our time. At best, those things cancel each other out.

Median family income adjusted for inflation was $29,000 in 1955.[28] In 2019 it was just over $62,000. We've used that wealth to live a life hardly conceivable to the 1950s American, even for a median family. The median American home increased from 983 square feet in 1950 to 2,436 square feet in 2018. The average new American home now has more bathrooms than occupants. Our cars are faster and more efficient, our TVs are cheaper and sharper.

What's happened to our time, on the other hand, barely looks like progress. And a lot of the reason has to do with the kind of jobs more of us now have.

John D. Rockefeller was one of the most successful businessmen of all time. He was also a recluse, spending most of his time by himself. He rarely spoke, deliberately making himself inaccessible and staying quiet when you caught his attention.

A refinery worker who occasionally had Rockefeller's ear once remarked: "He lets everybody else talk, while he sits back and says nothing."

When asked about his silence during meetings, Rockefeller often recited a poem:

> A wise old owl lived in an oak,
> The more he saw the less he spoke,
> The less he spoke, the more he heard,
> Why aren't we all like that wise old bird?

Rockefeller was a strange guy. But he figured out something that now applies to tens of millions of workers.

Rockefeller's job wasn't to drill wells, load trains, or move barrels. It was to think and make good decisions. Rockefeller's product—his deliverable—wasn't what he did with his hands, or even his words. It was what he figured out inside his head. So that's where he spent most of his time and energy. Despite sitting quietly most of the day in what might have looked like free time or leisure hours to most people, he was constantly working in his mind, thinking problems through.

This was unique in his day. Almost all jobs during Rockefeller's time required doing things with your hands. In 1870, 46% of jobs were in agriculture, and 35% were in crafts or manufacturing, according to economist Robert Gordon. Few professions relied on a worker's brain. You didn't think; you *labored*, without interruption, and your work was visible and tangible.

Today, that's flipped.

Thirty-eight percent of jobs are now designated as "managers, officials, and professionals." These are decision-making jobs. Another 41% are service jobs that often rely on your thoughts as much as your actions.

More of us have jobs that look closer to Rockefeller than a typical 1950s manufacturing worker, which means our days don't end when we clock out and leave the factory. We're constantly working in our heads, which means it feels like work never ends.

If your job is to build cars, there is little you can do when you're not on the assembly line. You detach from work and leave your tools in the factory. But if your job is to create a marketing campaign—a thought-based and decision job—your tool is your head, which never leaves you. You might be thinking about your project during your commute, as you're making dinner, while you put your kids to sleep, and when you wake up stressed at three in the morning. You might be on the clock for fewer hours than you would in 1950. But it feels like you're working 24/7.

Derek Thompson of *The Atlantic* once described it like this:

> If the operating equipment of the 21st century is a portable device, this means the modern factory is not a place at all. It is the day itself. The computer age has liberated the tools of productivity from the office. Most knowledge workers, whose laptops and smartphones are portable all-purpose media-making machines, can theoretically be as productive at 2 p.m. in the main office as at 2 a.m. in a Tokyo WeWork or at midnight on the couch.[29]

Compared to generations prior, control over your time has diminished. And since controlling your time is such a key happiness influencer, we shouldn't be surprised that people don't feel much happier even though we are, on average, richer than ever.

What do we do about that?

It's not an easy problem to solve, because everyone's different. The first step is merely acknowledging what does, and does not, make almost everyone happy.

In his book *30 Lessons for Living*, gerontologist Karl Pillemer interviewed a thousand elderly Americans looking for the most important lessons they learned from decades of life experience. He wrote:

> No one—not a single person out of a thousand—said that to be happy you should try to work as hard as you can to make money to buy the things you want.
>
> No one—not a single person—said it's important to be at least as wealthy as the people around you, and if you have more than they do it's real success.
>
> No one—not a single person—said you should choose your work based on your desired future earning power.

What they did value were things like quality friendships, being part of something bigger than themselves, and spending quality, unstructured time with their children. "Your kids don't want your money (or what your money buys) anywhere near as much as they want you. Specifically, they want you with them," Pillemer writes.

Take it from those who have lived through everything: Controlling your time is the highest dividend money pays.

Now, a short chapter on one of the lowest dividends money pays.

8.

Man in the Car Paradox

No one is impressed with your possessions as much as you are.

The best part of being a valet is getting to drive some of the coolest cars to ever touch pavement. Guests came in driving Ferraris, Lamborghinis, Rolls-Royces—the whole aristocratic fleet.

It was my dream to have one of these cars of my own, because (I thought) they sent such a strong signal to others that you made it. You're smart. You're rich. You have taste. You're important. *Look at me.*

The irony is that I rarely if ever looked at them, the drivers.

When you see someone driving a nice car, you rarely think, "Wow, the guy driving that car is cool." Instead, you think, "Wow, if *I* had that car people would think *I'm* cool." Subconscious or not, this is how people think.

There is a paradox here: people tend to want wealth to signal to others that they should be liked and admired. But in reality those other people often bypass admiring you, not because they don't think wealth is admirable, but because they use your wealth as a benchmark for their own desire to be liked and admired.

The letter I wrote after my son was born said, "You might think you want an expensive car, a fancy watch, and a huge house. But I'm telling you, you don't. What you want is respect and admiration from other people, and you think having expensive stuff will bring it. It almost never does—especially from the people you want to respect and admire you."

I learned that as a valet, when I began thinking about all the people driving up to the hotel in their Ferraris, watching me gawk. People must gawk everywhere they went, and I'm sure they loved it. I'm sure they felt admired.

But did they know I did not care about them, or even notice them? Did they know I was only gawking at the car, and imagining myself in the driver's seat?

Did they buy a Ferrari thinking it would bring them admiration without realizing that I—and likely most others—who are impressed with the car didn't actually give them, the driver, a moment's thought?

Does this same idea apply to those living in big homes? Almost certainly.

Jewelry and clothes? Yep.

My point here is not to abandon the pursuit of wealth. Or even fancy cars. I like both.

It's a subtle recognition that people generally aspire to be respected and admired by others, and using money to buy fancy things may bring less of it than you imagine. If respect and admiration are your goal, be careful how you seek it. Humility, kindness, and empathy will bring you more respect than horsepower ever will.

We're not done talking about Ferraris. Another story about the paradox of fast cars in the next chapter.

9.

Wealth is What You Don't See

Spending money to show people how much money you have is the fastest way to have less money.

MONEY HAS MANY ironies. Here's an important one: Wealth is what you don't see.

My time as a valet was in the mid-2000s in Los Angeles, when material appearance took precedence over everything but oxygen.

If you see a Ferrari driving around, you might intuitively assume the owner of the car is rich—even if you're not paying much attention to them. But as I got to know some of these people I realized that wasn't always the case. Many were mediocre successes who spent a huge percentage of their paycheck on a car.

I remember a fellow we'll call Roger. He was about my age. I had no idea what Roger did. But he drove a Porsche, which was enough for people to draw assumptions.

Then one day Roger arrived in an old Honda. Same the next week, and the next.

"What happened to your Porsche?" I asked. It was repossessed after defaulting on his car loan, he said. There was not a morsel of shame. He responded like he was telling the next play in the game. Every assumption you might have had about him was wrong. Los Angeles is full of Rogers.

Someone driving a $100,000 car might be wealthy. But the only data point you have about their wealth is that they have $100,000 less than they did before they bought the car (or $100,000 more in debt). That's *all* you know about them.

We tend to judge wealth by what we see, because that's the information we have in front of us. We can't see people's bank accounts or brokerage statements. So we rely on outward appearances to gauge financial success. Cars. Homes. Instagram photos.

Modern capitalism makes helping people fake it until they make it a cherished industry.

But the truth is that wealth is what you don't see.

Wealth is the nice cars not purchased. The diamonds not bought. The watches not worn, the clothes forgone and the first-class upgrade declined. Wealth is financial assets that haven't yet been converted into the stuff you see.

That's not how we think about wealth, because you can't contextualize what you can't see.

Singer Rihanna nearly went bankrupt after overspending and sued her financial advisor. The advisor responded: "Was it really necessary to tell her that if you spend money on things, you will end up with the things and not the money?"[30]

You can laugh, and please do. But the answer is, yes, people do need to be told that. When most people say they want to be a millionaire, what they might actually mean is "I'd like to spend a million dollars." And that is literally the opposite of being a millionaire.

Investor Bill Mann once wrote: "There is no faster way to feel rich than to spend lots of money on really nice things. But the way to be rich is to spend money you have, and to not spend money you don't have. It's really that simple."[31]

It is excellent advice, but it may not go far enough. The only way to be wealthy is to not spend the money that you do have. It's not just the only way to accumulate wealth; it's the very definition of wealth.

We should be careful to define the difference between *wealthy* and *rich*. It is more than semantics. Not knowing the difference is a source of countless poor money decisions.

Rich is a current income. Someone driving a $100,000 car is almost certainly rich, because even if they purchased the car with debt you need a certain level of income to afford the monthly payment. Same with those who live in big homes. It's not hard to spot rich people. They often go out of their way to make themselves known.

But *wealth* is hidden. It's income not spent. Wealth is an option not yet taken to buy something later. Its value lies in offering you options, flexibility, and growth to one day purchase more stuff than you could right now.

Diet and exercise offer a useful analogy. Losing weight is notoriously hard, even among those putting in the work of vigorous exercise. In his book *The Body*, Bill Bryson explains why:

> One study in America found that people overestimate the number of calories they burned in a workout by a factor of four. They also then consumed, on average, about twice as many calories as they had just burned off ... the fact is, you can quickly undo a lot of exercise by eating a lot of food, and most of us do.

Exercise is like being rich. You think, "I did the work and I now deserve to treat myself to a big meal." Wealth is turning down that treat meal and actually burning net calories. It's hard, and requires self-control. But it creates a gap between what you could do and what you choose to do that accrues to you over time.

The problem for many of us is that it is easy to find rich role models. It's harder to find wealthy ones because by definition their success is more hidden.

There are, of course, wealthy people who also spend a lot of money on stuff. But even in those cases what we see is their richness, not their wealth. We see the cars they chose to buy and perhaps the school they choose to send their kids to. We don't see the savings, retirement accounts, or investment portfolios. We see the homes they bought, not the homes they could have bought had they stretched themselves thin.

The danger here is that I think most people, deep down, want to be wealthy. They want freedom and flexibility, which is what financial assets not yet spent can give you. But it is so ingrained in us that to have money is to spend money that we don't get to see the restraint it takes to actually be wealthy. And since we can't see it, it's hard to learn about it.

People are good at learning by imitation. But the hidden nature of wealth makes it hard to imitate others and learn from their ways. After he died, Ronald Read became many people's financial role model. He was lionized in the media and cherished on social media. But he was nobody's financial role model while he was living because every penny of his wealth was hidden, even to those who knew him.

Imagine how hard it would be to learn how to write if you couldn't read the works of great authors. Who would be your inspiration? Who would you admire? Whose nuanced tricks and tips would you follow? It would make something that is already hard even harder. It's difficult to learn from what you can't see. Which helps explain why it's so hard for many to build wealth.

The world is filled with people who look modest but are actually wealthy and people who look rich who live at the razor's edge of insolvency. Keep this in mind when quickly judging others' success and setting your own goals.

If wealth is what you don't spend, what good is it? Well, let me convince you to save money.

10.

Save Money

The only factor you can control generates one of the only things that matters. How wonderful.

LET ME CONVINCE you to save money.

It won't take long.

But it's an odd task, isn't it?

Do people need to be convinced to save money?

My observation is that, yes, many do.

Past a certain level of income people fall into three groups: Those who save, those who don't think they can save, and those who don't think they need to save.

This is for the latter two.

The first idea—simple, but easy to overlook—is that building wealth has little to do with your income or investment returns, and lots to do with your savings rate.

A quick story about the power of efficiency.

In the 1970s the world looked like it was running out of oil. The calculation wasn't hard: The global economy used a lot of oil, the global economy was growing, and the amount of oil we could drill couldn't keep up.

We didn't run out of oil, thank goodness. But that wasn't just because we found more oil, or even got better at taking it out of the ground.

The biggest reason we overcame the oil crisis is because we started building cars, factories, and homes that are more energy efficient than they used to be. The United States uses 60% less energy per dollar of GDP today than it did in 1950.[32] The average miles per gallon of all vehicles on the road has doubled since 1975. A 1989 Ford Taurus (sedan) averaged 18.0 MPG. A 2019 Chevy Suburban (absurdly large SUV) averages 18.1 MPG.

The world grew its "energy wealth" not by increasing the energy it had, but by decreasing the energy it needed. U.S. oil and gas production has increased 65% since 1975, while conservation and efficiency has more than doubled what we can do with that energy. So it's easy to see which has mattered more.

The important thing here is that finding more energy is largely out of our control and shrouded in uncertainty, because it relies on a slippery mix of having the right geology, geography, weather, and geopolitics. But becoming more efficient with the energy we use is largely in our control. The decision to buy a lighter car or ride a bike is up to you and has a 100% chance of improving efficiency.

The same is true with our money.

Investment returns can make you rich. But whether an investing strategy will work, and how long it will work for, and whether markets will cooperate, is always in doubt. Results are shrouded in uncertainty.

Personal savings and frugality—finance's conservation and efficiency—are parts of the money equation that are more in your control and have a 100% chance of being as effective in the future as they are today.

If you view building wealth as something that will require more money or big investment returns, you may become as pessimistic as the energy doomers were in the 1970s. The path forward looks hard and out of your control.

If you view it as powered by your own frugality and efficiency, the destiny is clearer.

Wealth is just the accumulated leftovers after you spend what you take in. And since you can build wealth without a high income, but have no chance of building wealth without a high savings rate, it's clear which one matters more.

More importantly, the value of wealth is relative to what you need.

Say you and I have the same net worth.

And say you're a better investor than me. I can earn 8% annual returns and you can earn 12% annual returns.

But I'm more efficient with my money. Let's say I need half as much money to be happy while your lifestyle compounds as fast as your assets.

I'm better off than you are, despite being a worse investor. I'm getting more benefit from my investments despite lower returns.

The same is true for incomes. Learning to be happy with less money creates a gap between what you have and what you want—similar to the gap you get from growing your paycheck, but easier and more in your control.

A high savings rate means having lower expenses than you otherwise could, and having lower expenses means your savings go farther than they would if you spent more.

Think about this in the context of how much time and effort goes into achieving 0.1% of annual investment outperformance—millions of hours of research, tens of billions of dollars of effort from professionals—and it's easy to see what's potentially more important or worth chasing.

There are professional investors who grind 80 hours a week to add a tenth of a percentage point to their returns when there are two or three full percentage points of lifestyle bloat in their finances that can be exploited with less effort.

Big investment returns and fat paychecks are amazing when

they can be achieved, and some can achieve them. But the fact that there's so much effort put into one side of the finance equation and so little put into the other is an opportunity for most people.

Past a certain level of income, what you need is just what sits below your ego.

Everyone needs the basics. Once they're covered there's another level of comfortable basics, and past that there's basics that are both comfortable, entertaining, and enlightening.

But spending beyond a pretty low level of materialism is mostly a reflection of ego approaching income, a way to spend money to show people that you have (or had) money.

Think of it like this, and one of the most powerful ways to increase your savings isn't to raise your income. It's to raise your humility.

When you define savings as the gap between your ego and your income you realize why many people with decent incomes save so little. It's a daily struggle against instincts to extend your peacock feathers to their outermost limits and keep up with others doing the same.

People with enduring personal finance success—not necessarily those with high incomes—tend to have a propensity to not give a damn what others think about them.

So people's ability to save is more in their control than they might think.

Savings can be created by spending less.

You can spend less if you desire less.

And you will desire less if you care less about what others think of you.

As I argue often in this book, money relies more on psychology than finance.

And you don't need a specific reason to save.

Some people save money for a downpayment on a house, or a new car, or for retirement.

That's great, of course.

But saving does not require a goal of purchasing something specific.

You can save just for saving's sake. And indeed you should. Everyone should.

Only saving for a specific goal makes sense in a predictable world. But ours isn't. Saving is a hedge against life's inevitable ability to surprise the hell out of you at the worst possible moment.

Another benefit of savings that isn't attached to a spending goal is what we discussed in chapter 7: gaining control over your time.

Everyone knows the tangible stuff money buys. The intangible stuff is harder to wrap your head around, so it tends to go unnoticed. But the intangible benefits of money can be far more valuable and capable of increasing your happiness than the tangible things that are obvious targets of our savings.

Savings without a spending goal gives you options and flexibility, the ability to wait and the opportunity to pounce. It gives you time to think. It lets you change course on your own terms.

Every bit of savings is like taking a point in the future that would have been owned by someone else and giving it back to yourself.

That flexibility and control over your time is an unseen return on wealth.

What is the return on cash in the bank that gives you the option of changing careers, or retiring early, or freedom from worry?

I'd say it's incalculable.

It's incalculable in two ways. It's so large and important that we can't put a price on it. But it's also literally incalculable—we can't measure it like we can measure interest rates—and what we can't measure we tend to overlook.

When you don't have control over your time, you're forced to accept whatever bad luck is thrown your way. But if you have flexibility you have the time to wait for no-brainer opportunities to fall in your lap. This is a hidden return on your savings.

Savings in the bank that earn 0% interest might actually generate an extraordinary return if they give you the flexibility to take a job with a lower salary but more purpose, or wait for investment opportunities that come when those without flexibility turn desperate.

And that hidden return is becoming more important.

The world used to be hyper-local. Just over 100 years ago 75% of Americans had neither telephones nor regular mail service, according to historian Robert Gordon. That made competition hyper-local. A worker with just average intelligence might be the best in their town, and they got treated like the best because they didn't have to compete with the smarter worker in another town.

That's now changed.

A hyper-connected world means the talent pool you compete in has gone from hundreds or thousands spanning your town to millions or billions spanning the globe. This is especially true for jobs that rely on working with your head versus your muscles: teaching, marketing, analysis, consulting, accounting, programming, journalism, and even medicine increasingly compete in global talent pools. More fields will fall into this category as digitization erases global boundaries—as "software eats the world," as venture capitalist Marc Andreesen puts it.

A question you should ask as the range of your competition expands is, "How do I stand out?"

"I'm smart" is increasingly a bad answer to that question, because there are a lot of smart people in the world. Almost 600 people ace the SATs each year. Another 7,000 come within a handful of points. In a winner-take-all and globalized world these kinds of people are increasingly your direct competitors.

Intelligence is not a reliable advantage in a world that's become as connected as ours has.

But flexibility is.

In a world where intelligence is hyper-competitive and many previous technical skills have become automated, competitive advantages tilt toward nuanced and soft skills—like communication, empathy, and, perhaps most of all, flexibility.

If you have flexibility you can wait for good opportunities, both in your career and for your investments. You'll have a better chance of being able to learn a new skill when it's necessary. You'll feel less urgency to chase competitors who can do things you can't, and have more leeway to find your passion and your niche at your own pace. You can find a new routine, a slower pace, and think about life with a different set of assumptions. The ability to do those things when most others can't is one of the few things that will set you apart in a world where intelligence is no longer a sustainable advantage.

Having more control over your time and options is becoming one of the most valuable currencies in the world.

That's why more people can, and more people should, save money.

You know what else they should do? Stop trying to be so rational. Let me tell you why.

11.

Reasonable > Rational

Aiming to be mostly reasonable works better than trying to be coldly rational.

YOU'RE NOT A spreadsheet. You're a person. A screwed up, emotional person.

It took me a while to figure this out, but once it clicked I realized it's one of the most important parts of finance.

With it comes something that often goes overlooked: Do not aim to be coldly rational when making financial decisions. Aim to just be pretty reasonable. Reasonable is more realistic and you have a better chance of sticking with it for the long run, which is what matters most when managing money.

To show you what I mean, let me tell you the story of a guy who tried to cure syphilis with malaria.

Julius Wagner-Jauregg was a 19th-century psychiatrist with two unique skills: He was good at recognizing patterns, and what others saw as "crazy" he found merely "bold."

His specialty was patients with severe neurosyphilis—then a fatal diagnosis with no known treatment. He began noticing a pattern: syphilis patients tended to recover if they had the added misfortune of having prolonged fevers from an unrelated ailment.

Wagner-Jauregg assumed this was due to a hunch that had been around for centuries but doctors didn't understand well: fevers play a role in helping the body fight infection.

So he jumped to the logical conclusion.

In the early 1900s Wagner-Jauregg began injecting patients

with low-end strains of typhoid, malaria, and smallpox to trigger fevers strong enough to kill off their syphilis. This was as dangerous as it sounds. Some of his patients died from the treatment. He eventually settled on a weak version of malaria, since it could be effectively countered with quinine after a few days of bone-rattling fevers.

After some tragic trial and error his experiment worked. Wagner-Jauregg reported that 6 in 10 syphilis patients treated with "malariotherapy" recovered, compared to around 3 in 10 patients left alone. He won the Nobel Prize in medicine in 1927. The organization today notes: "The main work that concerned Wagner-Jauregg throughout his working life was the endeavour to cure mental disease by inducing a fever."[33]

Penicillin eventually made malariotherapy for syphilis patients obsolete, thank goodness. But Wagner-Jauregg is one of the only doctors in history who not only recognized fever's role in fighting infection, but also prescribed it as a treatment.

Fevers have always been as feared as they are mysterious. Ancient Romans worshiped Febris, the Goddess who protected people from fevers. Amulets were left at temples to placate her, hoping to stave off the next round of shivers.

But Wagner-Jauregg was onto something. Fevers are not accidental nuisances. They *do* play a role in the body's road to recovery. We now have better, more scientific evidence of fever's usefulness in fighting infection. A one-degree increase in body temperature has been shown to slow the replication rate of some viruses by a factor of 200. "Numerous investigators have identified a better outcome among patients who displayed fever," one NIH paper writes.[34] The Seattle Children's Hospital includes a section on its website to educate parents who may panic at the slightest rise in their child's temperature: "Fevers turn on the body's immune system. They help the body fight infection. Normal fevers between 100° and 104° F are good for sick children."[35]

But that's where the science ends and reality takes over.

Fever is almost universally seen as a bad thing. They're treated with drugs like Tylenol to reduce them as quickly as they appear. Despite millions of years of evolution as a defense mechanism, no parent, no patient, few doctors, and certainly no drug company views fever as anything but a misfortune that should be eliminated.

These views do not match the known science. One study was blunt: "Treatment of fever is common in the ICU setting and likely related to standard dogma rather than evidence-based practice."[36] Howard Markel, director of the Center for the History of Medicine, once said of fever phobia: "These are cultural practices that spread just as widely as the infectious diseases that are behind them."[37]

Why does this happen? If fevers are beneficial, why do we fight them so universally?

I don't think it's complicated: Fevers hurt. And people don't want to hurt.

That's it.

A doctor's goal is not just to cure disease. It's to cure disease within the confines of what's reasonable and tolerable to the patient. Fevers can have marginal benefits in fighting infection, but they hurt. And I go to the doctor to stop hurting. I don't care about double-blind studies when I'm shivering under a blanket. If you have a pill that can make a fever stop, give it to me now.

It may be rational to want a fever if you have an infection. But it's not reasonable.

That philosophy—aiming to be reasonable instead of rational—is one more people should consider when making decisions with their money.

Academic finance is devoted to finding the mathematically optimal investment strategies. My own theory is that, in the real world, people do not want the mathematically optimal strategy. They want the strategy that maximizes for how well they sleep at night.

Harry Markowitz won the Nobel Prize for exploring the mathematical tradeoff between risk and return. He was once asked how he invested his own money, and described his portfolio allocation in the 1950s, when his models were first developed:

> I visualized my grief if the stock market went way up and I wasn't in it—or if it went way down and I was completely in it. My intention was to minimize my future regret. So I split my contributions 50/50 between bonds and equities.

Markowitz eventually changed his investment strategy, diversifying the mix. But two things here are important.

One is that "minimizing future regret" is hard to rationalize on paper but easy to justify in real life. A rational investor makes decisions based on numeric facts. A reasonable investor makes them in a conference room surrounded by co-workers you want to think highly of you, with a spouse you don't want to let down, or judged against the silly but realistic competitors that are your brother-in-law, your neighbor, and your own personal doubts. Investing has a social component that's often ignored when viewed through a strictly financial lens.

The second is that *this is fine*. Jason Zweig, who conducted the interview when Markowitz described how he invested, later reflected:

> My own view is that people are neither rational nor irrational. We are human. We don't like to think harder than we need to, and we have unceasing demands on our attention. Seen in that light, there's nothing surprising about the fact that the pioneer of modern portfolio theory built his initial portfolio with so little regard for his own research. Nor is it surprising that he adjusted it later.[38]

Markowitz is neither rational or irrational. He's reasonable.

What's often overlooked in finance is that something can be technically true but contextually nonsense.

In 2008 a pair of researchers from Yale published a study arguing young savers should supercharge their retirement accounts using two-to-one margin (two dollars of debt for every dollar of their own money) when buying stocks. It suggests investors taper that leverage as they age, which lets a saver take more risk when they're young and can handle a magnified market rollercoaster, and less when they're older.

Even if using leverage left you wiped out when you were young (if you use two-to-one margin a 50% market drop leaves you with nothing) the researchers showed savers would still be better off in the long run so long as they picked themselves back up, followed the plan, and kept saving in a two-to-one leveraged account the day after being wiped out.

The math works on paper. It's a rational strategy.

But it's almost absurdly unreasonable.

No normal person could watch 100% of their retirement account evaporate and be so unphased that they carry on with the strategy undeterred. They'd quit, look for a different option, and perhaps sue their financial advisor.

The researchers argued that when using their strategy "the expected retirement wealth is 90% higher compared to life-cycle funds." It is also 100% less reasonable.

There is, in fact, a rational reason to favor what look like irrational decisions.

Here's one: Let me suggest that you love your investments.

This is not traditional advice. It's almost a badge of honor for investors to claim they're emotionless about their investments, because it seems rational.

But if lacking emotions about your strategy or the stocks you own increases the odds you'll walk away from them when they become difficult, what looks like rational thinking becomes a liability. The reasonable investors who love their technically imperfect strategies have an edge, because they're more likely to stick with those strategies.

There are few financial variables more correlated to performance than commitment to a strategy during its lean years—both the amount of performance and the odds of capturing it over a given period of time. The historical odds of making money in U.S. markets are 50/50 over one-day periods, 68% in one-year periods, 88% in 10-year periods, and (so far) 100% in 20-year periods. Anything that keeps you in the game has a quantifiable advantage.

If you view "do what you love" as a guide to a happier life, it sounds like empty fortune cookie advice. If you view it as the thing providing the endurance necessary to put the quantifiable odds of success in your favor, you realize it should be the most important part of any financial strategy.

Invest in a promising company you don't care about, and you might enjoy it when everything's going well. But when the tide inevitably turns you're suddenly losing money on something you're not interested in. It's a double burden, and the path of least resistance is to move onto something else. If you're passionate about the company to begin with—you love the mission, the product, the team, the science, whatever—the inevitable down times when you're losing money or the company needs help are blunted by the fact that at least you feel like you're part of something meaningful. That can be the necessary motivation that prevents you from giving up and moving on.

There are several other times when it's fine to be reasonable instead of rational with money.

There's a well-documented "home bias," where people prefer to invest in companies from the country they live in while ignoring the other 95%+ of the planet. It's not rational, until you consider that investing is effectively giving money to strangers. If familiarity helps you take the leap of faith required to remain backing those strangers, it's reasonable.

Day trading and picking individual stocks is not rational for most investors—the odds are heavily against your success. But they're both reasonable in small amounts if they scratch an itch hard enough to leave the rest of your more diversified investments alone. Investor Josh Brown, who advocates and mostly owns diversified funds, once explained why he also owns a smattering of individual stocks: "I'm not buying individual stocks because I think I'm going to generate alpha [outperformance]. I just love stocks and have ever since I was 20 years old. And it's my money, I get to do whatever." Quite reasonable.

Most forecasts about where the economy and the stock market are heading next are terrible, but making forecasts is reasonable. It's hard to wake up in the morning telling yourself you have no clue what the future holds, even if it's true. Acting on investment forecasts is dangerous. But I get why people try to predict what will happen next year. It's human nature. It's reasonable.

Jack Bogle, the late founder of Vanguard, spent his career on a crusade to promote low-cost passive index investing. Many thought it interesting that his son found a career as an active, high-fee hedge fund and mutual fund manager. Bogle—the man who said high-fee funds violate "the humble rules of arithmetic"—invested some of his own money in his son's funds. What's the explanation?

"We do some things for family reasons," Bogle told *The Wall Street Journal*. "If it's not consistent, well, life isn't always consistent."[39]

Indeed, it rarely is.

12.

Surprise!

History is the study of change, ironically used as a map of the future.

STANFORD PROFESSOR SCOTT SAGAN once said something everyone who follows the economy or investment markets should hang on their wall: "Things that have never happened before happen all the time."

History is mostly the study of surprising events. But it is often used by investors and economists as an unassailable guide to the future.

Do you see the irony?

Do you see the problem?

It is smart to have a deep appreciation for economic and investing history. History helps us calibrate our expectations, study where people tend to go wrong, and offers a rough guide of what tends to work. But it is not, in any way, a map of the future.

A trap many investors fall into is what I call "historians as prophets" fallacy: An overreliance on past data as a signal to future conditions in a field where innovation and change are the lifeblood of progress.

You can't blame investors for doing this. If you view investing as a hard science, history should be a perfect guide to the future. Geologists can look at a billion years of historical data and form models of how the earth behaves. So can meteorologists. And doctors—kidneys operate the same way in 2020 as they did in 1020.

But investing is not a hard science. It's a massive group of people making imperfect decisions with limited information about things that will have a massive impact on their wellbeing, which can make even smart people nervous, greedy and paranoid.

Richard Feynman, the great physicist, once said, "Imagine how much harder physics would be if electrons had feelings." Well, investors have feelings. Quite a few of them. That's why it's hard to predict what they'll do next based solely on what they did in the past.

The cornerstone of economics is that things change over time, because the invisible hand hates anything staying too good or too bad indefinitely. Investor Bill Bonner once described how Mr. Market works: "He's got a 'Capitalism at Work' T-shirt on and a sledgehammer in his hand." Few things stay the same for very long, which means we can't treat historians as prophets.

The most important driver of anything tied to money is the stories people tell themselves and the preferences they have for goods and services. Those things don't tend to sit still. They change with culture and generation. They're always changing and always will.

The mental trick we play on ourselves here is an over-admiration of people who have been there, done that, when it comes to money. Experiencing specific events does not necessarily qualify you to know what will happen next. In fact it rarely does, because experience leads to overconfidence more than forecasting ability.

Investor Michael Batnick once explained this well. Confronted with the argument that few investors are prepared for rising interest rates because they've never experienced them—the last big period of rising interest rates occurred almost 40 years ago—he argued that it didn't matter, because experiencing or even studying what happened in the past might not serve as any guide to what will happen when rates rise in the future:

> So what? Will the current rate hike look like the last one, or the one before that? Will different asset classes behave similarly, the same, or the exact opposite?

> On the one hand, people that have been investing through the events of 1987, 2000 and 2008 have experienced a lot of different markets. On the other hand, isn't it possible that this experience can lead to overconfidence? Failing to admit you're wrong? Anchoring to previous outcomes?

Two dangerous things happen when you rely too heavily on investment history as a guide to what's going to happen next.

1. You'll likely miss the outlier events that move the needle the most.

The most important events in historical data are the big outliers, the record-breaking events. They are what move the needle in the economy and the stock market. The Great Depression. World War II. The dot-com bubble. September 11th. The housing crash of the mid-2000s. A handful of outlier events play an enormous role because they influence so many unrelated events in their wake.

Fifteen billion people were born in the 19th and 20th centuries. But try to imagine how different the global economy—and the whole world—would be today if just seven of them never existed:

- Adolf Hitler
- Joseph Stalin
- Mao Zedong
- Gavrilo Princip
- Thomas Edison
- Bill Gates
- Martin Luther King

I'm not even sure that's the most meaningful list. But almost everything about the world today—from borders to technology to social norms—would be different if these seven people hadn't left their mark. Another way to put this is that 0.00000000004%

of people were responsible for perhaps the majority of the world's direction over the last century.

The same goes for projects, innovations, and events. Imagine the last century without:

- The Great Depression
- World War II
- The Manhattan Project
- Vaccines
- Antibiotics
- ARPANET
- September 11th
- The fall of the Soviet Union

How many projects and events occurred in the 20th century? Billions, trillions—who knows. But those eight alone impacted the world orders upon orders of magnitude more than others.

The thing that makes tail events easy to underappreciate is how easy it is to underestimate how things compound. How, for example, 9/11 prompted the Federal Reserve to cut interest rates, which helped drive the housing bubble, which led to the financial crisis, which led to a poor jobs market, which led tens of millions to seek a college education, which led to $1.6 trillion in student loans with a 10.8% default rate. It's not intuitive to link 19 hijackers to the current weight of student loans, but that's what happens in a world driven by a few outlier tail events.

The majority of what's happening at any given moment in the global economy can be tied back to a handful of past events that were nearly impossible to predict.

The most common plot of economic history is the role of surprises. The reason surprises occur is not because our models are wrong or our intelligence is low. It's because the odds that Adolf Hitler's parents argued on the evening nine months before he was born were the same as them conceiving a child. Technology is hard to predict because Bill Gates may have died from polio if Jonas Salk got cranky and gave up on his quest to find a vaccine. The reason we couldn't predict the student loan growth is because an airport security guard may have confiscated a hijacker's knife on 9/11. That's all there is to it.

The problem is that we often use events like the Great Depression and World War II to guide our views of things like worst-case scenarios when thinking about future investment returns. But those record-setting events had no precedent when they occurred. So the forecaster who assumes the worst (and best) events of the past will match the worst (and best) events of the future is not following history; they're accidentally assuming that the history of unprecedented events doesn't apply to the future.

Nassim Taleb writes in his book *Fooled By Randomness*:

> In Pharaonic Egypt … scribes tracked the high-water mark of the Nile and used it as an estimate for a future worst-case scenario. The same can be seen in the Fukushima nuclear reactor, which experienced a catastrophic failure in 2011 when a tsunami struck. It had been built to withstand the worst past historical earthquake, with the builders not imagining much worse—and not thinking that the worst past event had to be a surprise, as it had no precedent.

This is not a failure of analysis. It's a failure of imagination. Realizing the future might not look anything like the past is a special kind of skill that is not generally looked highly upon by the financial forecasting community.

At a 2017 dinner I attended in New York, Daniel Kahneman was asked how investors should respond when our forecasts are wrong. He said:

> Whenever we are surprised by something, even if we admit that

> we made a mistake, we say, 'Oh I'll never make that mistake again.' But, in fact, what you should learn when you make a mistake because you did not anticipate something is that the world is difficult to anticipate. That's the correct lesson to learn from surprises: that the world is surprising.

The correct lesson to learn from surprises is that the world is surprising. Not that we should use past surprises as a guide to future boundaries; that we should use past surprises as an admission that we have no idea what might happen next.

The most important economic events of the future—things that will move the needle the most—are things that history gives us little to no guide about. They will be unprecedented events. Their unprecedented nature means we won't be prepared for them, which is part of what makes them so impactful. This is true for both scary events like recessions and wars, and great events like innovation.

I'm confident in that prediction because surprises moving the needle the most is the one forecast that's been accurate at virtually every point in history.

2. History can be a misleading guide to the future of the economy and stock market because it doesn't account for structural changes that are relevant to today's world.

Consider a few big ones.

The 401(k) is 42 years old. The Roth IRA is younger, created in the 1990s. So personal financial advice and analysis about how Americans save for retirement today is not directly comparable to what made sense just a generation ago. We have new options. Things changed.

Or take venture capital. It barely existed 25 years ago. There are single venture capital funds today that are larger than the entire industry was a generation ago.[40] In his memoir, Nike founder Phil Knight wrote about his early days in business:

> There was no such thing as venture capital. An aspiring young entrepreneur had very few places to turn, and those places were all guarded by risk-averse gatekeepers with zero imagination. In other words, bankers.

What this means, in effect, is that all historical data going back just a few decades about how startups are financed is out of date. What we know about investment cycles and startup failure rates is not a deep base of history to learn from, because the way companies are funded today is such a new historical paradigm.

Or take public markets. The S&P 500 did not include financial stocks until 1976; today, financials make up 16% of the index. Technology stocks were virtually nonexistent 50 years ago. Today, they're more than a fifth of the index. Accounting rules have changed over time. So have disclosures, auditing, and the amount of market liquidity. Things changed.

The time between U.S. recessions has changed dramatically over the last 150 years:

The average time between recessions has grown from about two years in the late 1800s to five years in the early 20th century to eight years over the last half-century.

As I write this it looks like we're going into recession—12 years since the last recession began in December 2007. That's the longest gap between recessions since before the Civil War.

There are plenty of theories on why recessions have become less frequent. One is that the Fed is better at managing the business cycle, or at least extending it. Another is that heavy industry is more prone to boom-and-bust overproduction than the service industries that dominated the last 50 years. The pessimistic view is that we now have fewer recessions, but when they occur they are more powerful than before. For our argument it doesn't particularly matter what caused the change. What matters is that things clearly changed.

To show how these historic changes should affect investing decisions, consider the work of a man many believe to be one of the greatest investment minds of all time: Benjamin Graham.

Graham's classic book, *The Intelligent Investor*, is more than theory. It gives practical directions like formulas investors can use to make smart investing decisions.

I read Graham's book when I was a teenager, learning about investing for the first time. The formulas presented in the book were appealing to me, because they were literally step-by-step instructions on how to get rich. Just follow the instructions. It seemed so easy.

But something becomes clear when you try applying some of these formulas: few of them actually work.

Graham advocated purchasing stocks trading for less than their net working assets—basically cash in the bank minus all debts. This sounds great, but few stocks actually trade that cheaply anymore—other than, say, a penny stock accused of accounting fraud.

One of Graham's criteria instructs conservative investors to avoid stocks trading for more than 1.5 times book value. If you followed this rule over the last decade you would have owned almost nothing but insurance and bank stocks. There is no world where that is OK.

The Intelligent Investor is one of the greatest investing books of all time. But I don't know a single investor who has done well implementing Graham's published formulas. The book is full of wisdom—perhaps more than any other investment book ever published. But as a how-to guide, it's questionable at best.

What happened? Was Graham a showman who sounded good but whose advice didn't work? Not at all. He was a wildly successful investor himself.

But he was practical. And he was a true contrarian. He wasn't so wedded to investing ideas that he'd stick with them when too many other investors caught onto those theories, making them so popular as to render their potential useless. Jason Zweig—who annotated a later version of Graham's book—once wrote:

> Graham was constantly experimenting and retesting his assumptions and seeking out what works—not what worked yesterday but what works today. In each revised edition of *The Intelligent Investor,* Graham discarded the formulas he presented in the previous edition and replaced them with new ones, declaring, in a sense, that "those do not work anymore, or they do not work as well as they used to; these are the formulas that seem to work better now."
>
> One of the common criticisms made of Graham is that all the formulas in the 1972 edition are antiquated. The only proper response to this criticism is to say: "Of course they are! They are the ones he used to replace the formulas in the 1965 edition, which replaced the formulas in the 1954 edition, which, in turn, replaced the ones from the 1949 edition, which were

> used to augment the original formulas that he presented in *Security Analysis* in 1934."

Graham died in 1976. If the formulas he advocated were discarded and updated five times between 1934 and 1972, how relevant do you think they are in 2020? Or will be in 2050?

Just before he died Graham was asked whether detailed analysis of individual stocks—a tactic he became famous for—remained a strategy he favored. He answered:

> In general, no. I am no longer an advocate of elaborate techniques of security analysis in order to find superior value opportunities. This was a rewarding activity, say, 40 years ago, when our textbook was first published. But the situation has changed a great deal since then.[41]

What changed was: Competition grew as opportunities became well known; technology made information more accessible; and industries changed as the economy shifted from industrial to technology sectors, which have different business cycles and capital uses.

Things changed.

An interesting quirk of investing history is that the further back you look, the more likely you are to be examining a world that no longer applies to today. Many investors and economists take comfort in knowing their forecasts are backed up by decades, even centuries, of data. But since economies evolve, recent history is often the best guide to the future, because it's more likely to include important conditions that are relevant to the future.

There's a common phrase in investing, usually used mockingly, that "It's different this time." If you need to rebut someone who's predicting the future won't perfectly mirror the past, say, "Oh, so you think it's different this time?" and drop the mic. It comes from investor John Templeton's view that "The four most dangerous words in investing are, 'it's different this time.'"

Templeton, though, admitted that it is different at least 20% of the time. The world changes. Of course it does. And those changes are what matter most over time. Michael Batnick put it: "The twelve most dangerous words in investing are, 'The four most dangerous words in investing are, 'it's different this time.'"

That doesn't mean we should ignore history when thinking about money. But there's an important nuance: The further back in history you look, the more general your takeaways should be. General things like people's relationship to greed and fear, how they behave under stress, and how they respond to incentives tend to be stable in time. The history of money is useful for that kind of stuff.

But specific trends, specific trades, specific sectors, specific causal relationships about markets, and what people should do with their money are always an example of evolution in progress. Historians are not prophets.

The question, then, is how should we think about and plan for the future? Let's take a look in the next chapter.

13.

Room for Error

The most important part of every plan is planning on your plan not going according to plan.

SOME OF THE best examples of smart financial behavior can be found in an unlikely place: Las Vegas casinos.

Not among all players, of course. But a tiny group of blackjack players who practice card counting can teach ordinary people something extraordinarily important about managing money: the importance of room for error.

The fundamentals of blackjack card counting are simple:

- No one can know with certainty what card the dealer will draw next.
- But by tracking what cards have already been dealt you can calculate what cards remain in the deck.
- Doing so can tell you *the odds* of a particular card being drawn by the dealer.

As a player, you bet more when the odds of getting a card you want are in your favor and less when they are against you.

The mechanics of how this is done don't matter here. What matters is that a blackjack card counter knows they are playing a game of odds, not certainties. In any particular hand they think they have a good chance of being right, but know there's a decent chance they're wrong. It might sound strange given their profession, but their strategy relies entirely on humility—

humility that they don't know, and cannot know exactly what's going to happen next, so play their hand accordingly. The card counting system works because it tilts the odds ever so slightly from the house to the player. But bet too heavily even when the odds seem in your favor and, if you're wrong, you might lose so much that you don't have enough money to keep playing.

There is never a moment when you're so right that you can bet every chip in front of you. The world isn't that kind to anyone—not consistently, anyways. You have to give yourself room for error. You have to plan on your plan not going according to plan.

Kevin Lewis, a successful card counter portrayed in the book *Bringing Down the House*, wrote more about this philosophy:

> Although card counting is statistically proven to work, it does not guarantee you will win every hand—let alone every trip you make to the casino. We must make sure that we have enough money to withstand any swings of bad luck.
>
> Let's assume you have roughly a 2 percent edge over the casino. That still means the casino will win 49 percent of the time. Therefore, you need to have enough money to withstand any variant swings against you. A rule of thumb is that you should have at least a hundred basic units. Assuming you start with ten thousand dollars, you could comfortably play a hundred-dollar unit.

History is littered with good ideas taken too far, which are indistinguishable from bad ideas. The wisdom in having room for error is acknowledging that uncertainty, randomness, and chance—"unknowns"—are an ever-present part of life. The only way to deal with them is by increasing the gap between what you think will happen and what *can* happen while still leaving you capable of fighting another day.

Benjamin Graham is known for his concept of margin of safety. He wrote about it extensively and in mathematical detail. But my favorite summary of the theory came when he mentioned in an interview that "the purpose of the margin of safety is to render the forecast unnecessary."

It's hard to overstate how much power lies in that simple statement.

Margin of safety—you can also call it room for error or redundancy—is the only effective way to safely navigate a world that is governed by odds, not certainties. And almost everything related to money exists in that kind of world.

Forecasting with precision is hard. This is obvious to the card counter, because no one could possibly know where a particular card lies in a shuffled deck. It's less obvious to someone asking, "What will the average annual return of the stock market be over the next 10 years?" or "On what date will I be able to retire?" But they are fundamentally the same. The best we can do is think about odds.

Graham's margin of safety is a simple suggestion that we don't need to view the world in front of us as black or white, predictable or a crapshoot. The grey area—pursuing things where a range of potential outcomes are acceptable—is the smart way to proceed.

But people underestimate the need for room for error in almost everything they do that involves money. Stock analysts give their clients price targets, not price ranges. Economic forecasters predict things with precise figures; rarely broad probabilities. The pundit who speaks in unshakable certainties will gain a larger following than the one who says "We can't know for sure," and speaks in probabilities.[42]

We do this in all kinds of financial endeavors, especially those related to our own decisions. Harvard psychologist Max Bazerman once showed that when analyzing other people's home renovation plans, most people estimate the project will run between 25% and 50% over budget.[43] But when it comes to their own projects, people estimate that renovations will be completed on time and at budget. Oh, the eventual disappointment.

Two things cause us to avoid room for error. One is the idea that somebody must know what the future holds, driven by the uncomfortable feeling that comes from admitting the opposite. The second is that you're therefore doing yourself harm by not taking actions that fully exploit an accurate view of that future coming true.

But room for error is underappreciated and misunderstood. It's often viewed as a conservative hedge, used by those who don't want to take much risk or aren't confident in their views. But when used appropriately, it's quite the opposite.

Room for error lets you endure a range of potential outcomes, and endurance lets you stick around long enough to let the odds of benefiting from a low-probability outcome fall in your favor. The biggest gains occur infrequently, either because they don't happen often or because they take time to compound. So the person with enough room for error in part of their strategy (cash) to let them endure hardship in another (stocks) has an edge over the person who gets wiped out, game over, insert more tokens, when they're wrong.

Bill Gates understood this well. When Microsoft was a young company, he said he "came up with this incredibly conservative approach that I wanted to have enough money in the bank to pay a year's worth of payroll even if we didn't get any payments coming in." Warren Buffett expressed a similar idea when he told Berkshire Hathaway shareholders in 2008: "I have pledged—to you, the rating agencies and myself—to always run Berkshire with more than ample cash ... When forced to choose, I will not trade even a night's sleep for the chance of extra profits."[44]

There are a few specific places for investors to think about room for error.

One is volatility. Can you survive your assets declining by 30%? On a spreadsheet, maybe yes—in terms of actually paying your bills and staying cash-flow positive. But what about mentally? It is easy to underestimate what a 30% decline does to your psyche. Your confidence may become shot at the very moment opportunity is at its highest. You—or your spouse—may decide it's time for a new plan, or new career. I know several investors who quit after losses because they were exhausted. Physically exhausted. Spreadsheets are good at telling you when the numbers do or don't add up. They're not good at modeling how you'll feel when you tuck your kids in at night wondering if the investment decisions you've made were a mistake that will hurt their future. Having a gap between what you can technically endure versus what's emotionally possible is an overlooked version of room for error.

Another is saving for retirement. We can look at history and see, for example, that the U.S. stock market has returned an annual average of 6.8% after inflation since the 1870s. It's a reasonable first approximation to use that as an estimate of what to expect on your own diversified portfolio when saving for retirement. You can use those return assumptions to back into the amount of money you'll need to save each month to achieve your target nestegg.

But what if future returns are lower? Or what if long-term history is a good estimate of the long-term future, but your target retirement date ends up falling in the middle of a brutal bear market, like 2009? What if a future bear market scares you out of stocks and you end up missing a future bull market, so the returns you actually earn are less than the market average? What if you need to cash out your retirement accounts in your 30s to pay for a medical mishap?

The answer to those what ifs is, "You won't be able to retire like you once predicted." Which can be a disaster.

The solution is simple: Use room for error when estimating your future returns. This is more art than science. For my own investments, which I'll describe more in chapter 20, I assume the future returns I'll earn in my lifetime will be ⅓ lower than the historic average. So I save more than I would if I assumed the future will resemble the past. It's my margin of safety. The future may be worse than ⅓ lower than the past, but no margin of safety offers a 100% guarantee. A one-third buffer is enough to allow me to sleep well at night. And if the future does resemble the past, I'll be pleasantly surprised. "The best way to achieve felicity is to aim low," says Charlie Munger. Wonderful.

An important cousin of room for error is what I call optimism bias in risk-taking, or "Russian roulette should statistically work" syndrome: An attachment to favorable odds when the downside is unacceptable in any circumstances.

Nassim Taleb says, "You can be risk loving and yet completely averse to ruin." And indeed, you should.

The idea is that you have to take risk to get ahead, but no risk that can wipe you out is ever worth taking. The odds are in your favor when playing Russian roulette. But the downside is not worth the potential upside. There is no margin of safety that can compensate for the risk.

Same with money. The odds of many lucrative things are in your favor. Real estate prices go up most years, and during most years you'll get a paycheck every other week. But if something has 95% odds of being right, the 5% odds of being wrong means you will almost certainly experience the downside at some point in your life. And if the cost of the downside is ruin, the upside the other 95% of the time likely isn't worth the risk, no matter how appealing it looks.

Leverage is the devil here. Leverage—taking on debt to make

your money go further—pushes routine risks into something capable of producing ruin. The danger is that rational optimism most of the time masks the odds of ruin some of the time. The result is we systematically underestimate risk. Housing prices fell 30% last decade. A few companies defaulted on their debt. That's capitalism. It happens. But those with high leverage had a double wipeout: Not only were they left broke, but being wiped out erased every opportunity to get back in the game at the very moment opportunity was ripe. A homeowner wiped out in 2009 had no chance of taking advantage of cheap mortgage rates in 2010. Lehman Brothers had no chance of investing in cheap debt in 2009. They were done.

To get around this, I think of my own money as barbelled. I take risks with one portion and am terrified with the other. This is not inconsistent, but the psychology of money would lead you to believe that it is. I just want to ensure I can remain standing long enough for my risks to pay off. You have to survive to succeed. To repeat a point we've made a few times in this book: The ability to do what you want, when you want, for as long as you want, has an infinite ROI.

Room for error does more than just widen the target around what you think might happen. It also helps protect you from things you'd never imagine, which can be the most troublesome events we face.

The Battle of Stalingrad during World War II was the largest battle in history. With it came equally staggering stories of how people dealt with risk.

One came in late 1942, when a German tank unit sat in reserve on grasslands outside the city. When tanks were desperately needed on the front lines, something happened that surprised everyone: Almost none of them worked.

Out of 104 tanks in the unit, fewer than 20 were operable. Engineers quickly found the issue. Historian William Craig writes: "During the weeks of inactivity behind the front lines, field mice had nested inside the vehicles and eaten away insulation covering the electrical systems."

The Germans had the most sophisticated equipment in the world. Yet there they were, defeated by mice.

You can imagine their disbelief. This almost certainly never crossed their minds. What kind of tank designer thinks about mouse protection? Not a reasonable one. And not one who studied tank history.

But these kinds of things happen all the time. You can plan for every risk except the things that are too crazy to cross your mind. And those crazy things can do the most harm, because they happen more often than you think and you have no plan for how to deal with them.

In 2006 Warren Buffett announced a search for his eventual replacement. He said he needed someone "genetically programmed to recognize and avoid serious risks, including those never before encountered."[45]

I have seen this skill at work with startups my firm, Collaborative Fund, has backed. Ask a founder to list the biggest risks they face, and the usual suspects are mentioned. But beyond the predictable struggles of running a startup, here are a few issues we've dealt with among our portfolio companies:

- Water pipes broke, flooding and ruining a company's office.
- A company's office was broken into three times.
- A company was kicked out of its manufacturing plant.
- A store was shut down after a customer called the health department because she didn't like that another customer brought a dog inside.

- A CEO's email was spoofed in the middle of a fundraise that required all of his attention.
- A founder had a mental breakdown.

Several of these events were existential to the company's future. But none were foreseeable, because none had previously happened to the CEOs dealing with these problems—or anyone else they knew, for that matter. It was unchartered territory.

Avoiding these kinds of unknown risks is, almost by definition, impossible. You can't prepare for what you can't envision.

If there's one way to guard against their damage, it's avoiding single points of failure.

A good rule of thumb for a lot of things in life is that everything that can break will eventually break. So if many things rely on one thing working, and that thing breaks, you are counting the days to catastrophe. That's a single point of failure.

Some people are remarkably good at avoiding single points of failure. Most critical systems on airplanes have backups, and the backups often have backups. Modern jets have four redundant electrical systems. You can fly with one engine and technically land with none, as every jet must be capable of stopping on a runway with its brakes alone, without thrust reverse from its engines. Suspension bridges can similarly lose many of their cables without falling.

The biggest single point of failure with money is a sole reliance on a paycheck to fund short-term spending needs, with no savings to create a gap between what you think your expenses are and what they might be in the future.

The trick that often goes overlooked—even by the wealthiest—is what we saw in chapter 10: realizing that you don't need a specific reason to save. It's fine to save for a car, or a home, or for retirement. But it's equally important to save for things you can't possibly predict or even comprehend—the financial equivalent of field mice.

Predicting what you'll use your savings for assumes you live in a world where you know exactly what your future expenses will be, which no one does. I save a lot, and I have no idea what I'll use the savings for in the future. Few financial plans that only prepare for known risks have enough margin of safety to survive the real world.

In fact, the most important part of every plan is planning on your plan not going according to plan.

Now, let me show you how this applies to you.

14.

You'll Change

Long-term planning is harder than it seems because people's goals and desires change over time.

I grew up with a friend who came from neither privilege nor natural intellect, but was the hardest-working guy I knew. These people have a lot to teach because they have an unfiltered understanding of every inch of the road to success.

His life's mission and dream as a teenager was to be a doctor. To say the odds were stacked against him is being charitable. No reasonable person at the time would consider it a possibility.

But he pushed. And—a decade older than his classmates—he eventually became a doctor.

How much fulfillment comes from starting from nothing, bulldozing your way to the top of medical school, and achieving one of the most noble professions against all odds?

I spoke to him a few years ago. The conversation went like this:

Me: "Long time no talk! How you doi—"

Him: "Awful career."

Me: "Haha, well—"

Him: "Awful career, man."

This went on for 10 minutes. The stress and hours had worn him into the ground. He seemed as disappointed in where he is today as he was driven toward where he wanted to be 15 years ago.

An underpinning of psychology is that people are poor forecasters of their future selves.

Imagining a goal is easy and fun. Imagining a goal in the context of the realistic life stresses that grow with competitive pursuits is something entirely different.

This has a big impact on our ability to plan for future financial goals.

Every five-year-old boy wants to drive a tractor when they grow up. Few jobs look better in the eyes of a young boy whose idea of a good job begins and ends with "Vroom vroom, beep beep, big tractor, here I come!"

Then many grow up and realize that driving a tractor maybe isn't the best career. Maybe they want something more prestigious or lucrative.

So as a teenager they dream of being a lawyer. Now they think—they *know*—their plan is set. Law school and its costs, here we come.

Then, as a lawyer, they face such long working hours that they rarely see their families.

So perhaps they take a lower-paying job with flexible hours. Then they realize that childcare is so expensive that it consumes most of their paycheck, and they opt to be a stay-at-home parent. This, they conclude, is finally the right choice.

Then, at age 70, they realize that a lifetime of staying home means they're unprepared to afford retirement.

Many of us wind through life on a similar trajectory. Only 27% of college grads have a job related to their major, according to the Federal Reserve.[46] Twenty-nine percent of stay-at-home parents have a college degree.[47] Few likely regret their education, of course. But we should acknowledge that a new parent in their 30s may think about life goals in a way their 18-year-old self making career goals would never imagine.

Long-term financial planning is essential. But things change—both the world around you, and your own goals and desires. It is one thing to say, "We don't know what the future holds." It's another to admit that you, yourself, don't know today what you will even want in the future. And the truth is, few of us do. It's hard to make enduring long-term decisions when your view of what you'll want in the future is likely to shift.

The End of History Illusion is what psychologists call the tendency for people to be keenly aware of how much they've changed in the past, but to underestimate how much their personalities, desires, and goals are likely to change in the future. Harvard psychologist Daniel Gilbert once said:

> At every stage of our lives we make decisions that will profoundly influence the lives of the people we're going to become, and then when we become those people, we're not always thrilled with the decisions we made. So young people pay good money to get tattoos removed that teenagers paid good money to get. Middle-aged people rushed to divorce people who young adults rushed to marry. Older adults work hard to lose what middle-aged adults worked hard to gain. On and on and on.[48]

"All of us," he said, "are walking around with an illusion—an illusion that history, our personal history, has just come to an end, that we have just recently become the people that we were always meant to be and will be for the rest of our lives." We tend to never learn this lesson. Gilbert's research shows people from age 18 to 68 underestimate how much they will change in the future.

You can see how this can impact a long-term financial plan. Charlie Munger says the first rule of compounding is to *never interrupt it unnecessarily*. But how do you not interrupt a money plan—careers, investments, spending, budgeting, whatever—when what you want out of life changes? It's hard. Part of the reason people like Ronald Read—the wealthy janitor we met earlier in the book—and Warren Buffett become so successful is because they kept doing the same thing for decades on end, letting compounding run wild. But many of us evolve so much over a lifetime that we don't want to keep doing the same thing for decades on end. Or anything close to it. So rather than one 80-something-year lifespan, our money has perhaps four distinct 20-year blocks.

I know young people who purposefully live austere lives with little income, and they're perfectly happy with it. Then there are those who work their tails off to pay for a life of luxury, and they're perfectly happy with that. Both have risks—the former risks being unprepared to raise a family or fund retirement, the latter risks regret that you spent your youthful and healthy years in a cubicle.

There is no easy solution to this problem. Tell a five-year-old boy he should be a lawyer instead of a tractor driver and he will disagree with every cell in his body.

But there are two things to keep in mind when making what you think are long-term decisions.

We should avoid the extreme ends of financial planning. Assuming you'll be happy with a very low income, or choosing to work endless hours in pursuit of a high one, increases the odds that you'll one day find yourself at a point of regret. The fuel of the End of History Illusion is that people adapt to most circumstances, so the benefits of an extreme plan—the simplicity of having hardly anything, or the thrill of having almost everything—wear off. But the downsides of those extremes—not being able to afford retirement, or looking back at a life spent devoted to chasing dollars—become enduring regrets. Regrets are especially painful when you abandon a previous plan and feel like you have to run in the other direction twice as fast to make up for lost time.

Compounding works best when you can give a plan years or decades to grow. This is true for not only savings but careers and relationships. Endurance is key. And when you consider our tendency to change who we are over time, balance at every point in your life becomes a strategy to avoid future regret and encourage endurance.

Aiming, at every point in your working life, to have moderate annual savings, moderate free time, no more than a moderate commute, and at least moderate time with your family, increases the odds of being able to stick with a plan and avoid regret than if any one of those things fall to the extreme sides of the spectrum.

We should also come to accept the reality of changing our minds. Some of the most miserable workers I've met are people who stay loyal to a career only because it's the field they picked when deciding on a college major at age 18. When you accept the End of History Illusion, you realize that the odds of picking a job when you're not old enough to drink that you will still enjoy when you're old enough to qualify for Social Security are low.

The trick is to accept the reality of change and move on as soon as possible.

Jason Zweig, the *Wall Street Journal* investment columnist, worked with psychologist Daniel Kahneman on writing Kahneman's book *Thinking, Fast and Slow*. Zweig once told a story about a personality quirk of Kahneman's that served him well: "Nothing amazed me more about Danny than his ability to detonate what we had just done," Zweig wrote. He and Kahneman could work endlessly on a chapter, but:

> The next thing you know, [Kahneman] sends a version so utterly transformed that it is unrecognizable: It begins differently, it ends differently, it incorporates anecdotes and evidence you never would have thought of, it draws on research that you've never heard of.

"When I asked Danny how he could start again as if we had never written an earlier draft," Zweig continued, "he said the words I've never forgotten: 'I have no sunk costs.'"[49]

Sunk costs—anchoring decisions to past efforts that can't be refunded—are a devil in a world where people change over time. They make our future selves prisoners to our past, different, selves. It's the equivalent of a stranger making major life decisions for you.

Embracing the idea that financial goals made when you were a different person should be abandoned without mercy versus put on life support and dragged on can be a good strategy to minimize future regret.

The quicker it's done, the sooner you can get back to compounding.

Next, let's talk about compounding's price of admission.

15.

Nothing's Free

Everything has a price, but not all prices appear on labels.

EVERYTHING HAS A price, and the key to a lot of things with money is just figuring out what that price is and being willing to pay it.

The problem is that the price of a lot of things is not obvious until you've experienced them firsthand, when the bill is overdue.

General Electric was the largest company in the world in 2004, worth a third of a trillion dollars. It had either been first or second each year for the previous decade, capitalism's shining example of corporate aristocracy.

Then everything fell to pieces.

The 2008 financial crisis sent GE's financing division—which supplied more than half the company's profits—into chaos. It was eventually sold for scrap. Subsequent bets in oil and energy were disasters, resulting in billions in writeoffs. GE stock fell from $40 in 2007 to $7 by 2018.

Blame placed on CEO Jeff Immelt—who ran the company since 2001—was immediate and harsh. He was criticized for his leadership, his acquisitions, cutting the dividend, laying off workers and—of course—the plunging stock price. Rightly so: those rewarded with dynastic wealth when times are good hold the burden of responsibility when the tide goes out. He stepped down in 2017.

But Immelt said something insightful on his way out.

Responding to critics who said his actions were wrong and what he should have done was obvious, Immelt told his successor, "Every job looks easy when you're not the one doing it."

Every job looks easy when you're not the one doing it because the challenges faced by someone in the arena are often invisible to those in the crowd.

Dealing with the conflicting demands of sprawling bloat, short-term investors, regulators, unions, and entrenched bureaucracy is not only hard to do, but it's hard to even recognize the severity of the problems until you're the one dealing with them. Immelt's successor, who lasted 14 months, learned this as well.

Most things are harder in practice than they are in theory. Sometimes this is because we're overconfident. More often it's because we're not good at identifying what the price of success is, which prevents us from being able to pay it.

The S&P 500 increased 119-fold in the 50 years ending 2018. All you had to do was sit back and let your money compound. But, of course, successful investing looks easy when you're not the one doing it.

"Hold stocks for the long run," you'll hear. It's good advice.

But do you know how hard it is to maintain a long-term outlook when stocks are collapsing?

Like everything else worthwhile, successful investing demands a price. But its currency is not dollars and cents. It's volatility, fear, doubt, uncertainty, and regret—all of which are easy to overlook until you're dealing with them in real time.

The inability to recognize that investing has a price can tempt us to try to get something for nothing. Which, like shoplifting, rarely ends well.

Say you want a new car. It costs $30,000. You have three options: 1) Pay $30,000 for it, 2) find a cheaper used one, or 3) steal it. In this case, 99% of people know to avoid the third option, because the consequences of stealing a car outweigh the upside.

But say you want to earn an 11% annual return over the next 30 years so you can retire in peace. Does this reward come free? Of course not. The world is never that nice. There's a price tag, a bill that must be paid. In this case it's a never-ending taunt from the market, which gives big returns and takes them away just as fast. Including dividends the Dow Jones Industrial Average returned about 11% per year from 1950 to 2019, which is great. But the price of success during this period was dreadfully high. The shaded lines in the chart show when it was at least 5% below its previous all-time high.

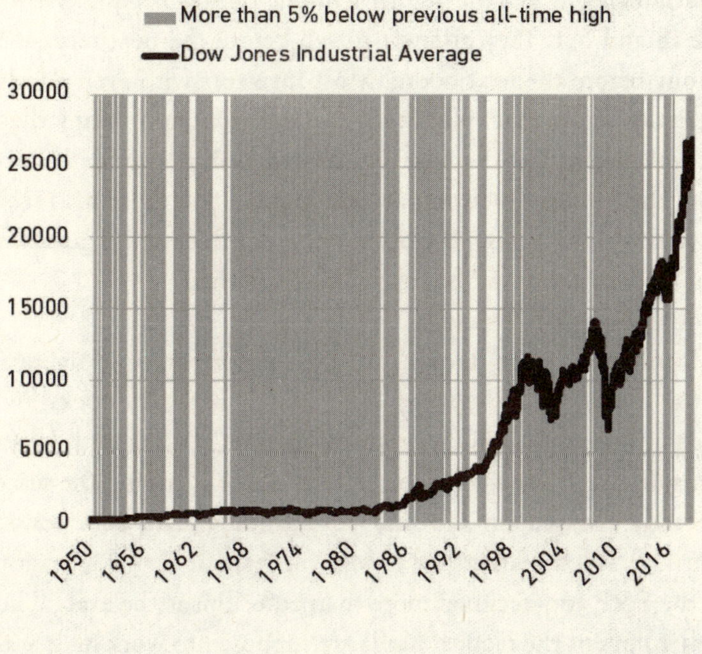

This is the price of market returns. The fee. It is the cost of admission. And it hurts.

Like most products, the bigger the returns, the higher the price. Netflix stock returned more than 35,000% from 2002 to 2018, but traded below its previous all-time high on 94% of days. Monster Beverage returned 319,000% from 1995 to 2018—among the highest returns in history—but traded below its previous high 95% of the time during that period.

Now here's the important part. Like the car, you have a few options: You can pay this price, accepting volatility and upheaval. Or you can find an asset with less uncertainty and a lower payoff, the equivalent of a used car. Or you can attempt the equivalent of grand-theft auto: Try to get the return while avoiding the volatility that comes along with it.

Many people in investing choose the third option. Like a car thief—though well-meaning and law-abiding—they form tricks and strategies to get the return without paying the price. They trade in and out. They attempt to sell before the next recession and buy before the next boom. Most investors with even a little experience know that volatility is real and common. Many then take what seems like the next logical step: trying to avoid it.

But the Money Gods do not look highly upon those who seek a reward without paying the price. Some car thieves will get away with it. Many more will be caught and punished.

Same thing with investing.

Morningstar once looked at the performance of tactical mutual funds, whose strategy is to switch between stocks and bonds at opportune times, capturing market returns with lower downside risk.[50] They want the returns without paying the price. The study focused on the mid-2010 through late 2011 period, when U.S. stock markets went wild on fears of a new recession and the S&P 500 declined more than 20%. This is the exact kind of environment the tactical funds are supposed to work in. It was their moment to shine.

There were, by Morningstar's count, 112 tactical mutual funds during this period. Only nine had better risk-adjusted returns than a simple 60/40 stock-bond fund. Less than a quarter of the tactical funds had smaller maximum drawdowns than the leave-it-alone index. Morningstar wrote: "With a few exceptions, [tactical funds] gained less, were more volatile, or were subject to just as much downside risk" as the hands-off fund.

Individual investors fall for this when making their own investments, too. The average equity fund investor underperformed the funds they invested in by half a percent per year, according to Morningstar—the result of buying and selling when they should have just bought and held.[51]

The irony is that by trying to avoid the price, investors end up paying double.

Back to GE. One of its many faults stems from an era under former CEO Jack Welch. Welch became famous for ensuring quarterly earnings per share beat Wall Street estimates. He was the grandmaster. If Wall Street analysts expected $0.25 per share, Jack would deliver $0.26 no matter the state of business or the economy. He'd do that by massaging the numbers—that description is charitable—often pulling gains from future quarters into the current quarter to make the obedient numbers salute their master.

Forbes reported one of dozens of examples: "[General Electric] for two years in a row 'sold' locomotives to unnamed financial partners instead of end users in transactions that left most of the risks of ownership with GE."[52]

Welch never denied this game. He wrote in his book *Straight From the Gut*:

> The response of our business leaders to the crises was typical of the GE culture. Even though the books had closed on the quarter, many immediately offered to pitch in to cover the [earnings] gap. Some said they could find an extra $10 million, $20 million, and even $30 million from their business to offset the surprise.

The result was that under Welch's leadership, stockholders didn't have to pay the price. They got consistency and predictability—a stock that surged year after year without the surprises of uncertainty. Then the bill came due, like it always does. GE shareholders have suffered through a decade of mammoth losses that were previously shielded by accounting maneuvers. The penny gains of Welch's era became dime losses today.

The strangest example of this comes from failed mortgage giants Freddie Mac and Fannie Mae, which in the early 2000s were caught *under-reporting* current earnings by billions of dollars with the intention of spreading those gains out over future periods to give investors the illusion of smoothness and predictability.[53] The illusion of not having to pay the price.

The question is: Why do so many people who are willing to pay the price of cars, houses, food, and vacations try so hard to avoid paying the price of good investment returns?

The answer is simple: The price of investing success is not immediately obvious. It's not a price tag you can see, so when the bill comes due it doesn't feel like a fee for getting something good. It feels like a fine for doing something wrong. And while people are generally fine with paying fees, fines are supposed to be avoided. You're supposed to make decisions that preempt and avoid fines. Traffic fines and IRS fines mean you did something wrong and deserve to be punished. The natural response for anyone who watches their wealth decline and views that drop as a fine is to avoid future fines.

It sounds trivial, but thinking of market volatility as a fee rather than a fine is an important part of developing the kind of mindset that lets you stick around long enough for investing gains to work in your favor.

Few investors have the disposition to say, "I'm actually fine if I lose 20% of my money." This is doubly true for new investors who have never experienced a 20% decline.

But if you view volatility as a fee, things look different.

Disneyland tickets cost $100. But you get an awesome day with your kids you'll never forget. Last year more than 18 million people thought that fee was worth paying. Few felt the $100 was a punishment or a fine. The worthwhile tradeoff of fees is obvious when it's clear you're paying one.

Same with investing, where volatility is almost always a fee, not a fine.

Market returns are never free and never will be. They demand you pay a price, like any other product. You're not forced to pay this fee, just like you're not forced to go to Disneyland. You can go to the local county fair where tickets might be $10, or stay home for free. You might still have a good time. But you'll usually get what you pay for. Same with markets. The volatility/uncertainty fee—the price of returns—is the cost of admission to get returns greater than low-fee parks like cash and bonds.

The trick is convincing yourself that the market's fee is worth it. That's the only way to properly deal with volatility and uncertainty—not just putting up with it, but realizing that it's an admission fee worth paying.

There's no guarantee that it will be. Sometimes it rains at Disneyland.

But if you view the admission fee as a fine, you'll never enjoy the magic.

Find the price, then pay it.

16.

You & Me

Beware taking financial cues from people playing a different game than you are.

THE IMPLOSION OF the dot-com bubble in the early 2000s reduced household wealth by $6.2 trillion.

The end of the housing bubble cut away more than $8 trillion.

It's hard to overstate how socially devastating financial bubbles can be. They ruin lives.

Why do these things happen?

And why do they *keep* happening?

Why can't we learn our lessons?

The common answer here is that people are greedy, and greed is an indelible feature of human nature.

That may be true, and it's a good enough answer for most. But remember from chapter 1: no one is crazy. People make financial decisions they regret, and they often do so with scarce information and without logic. But the decisions made sense to them when they were made. Blaming bubbles on greed and stopping there misses important lessons about how and why people rationalize what in hindsight look like greedy decisions.

Part of why bubbles are hard to learn from is that they are not like cancer, where a biopsy gives us a clear warning and diagnosis. They are closer to the rise and fall of a political party, where the outcome is known in hindsight but the cause and blame are never agreed upon.

Competition for investment returns is fierce, and someone has to own every asset at every point in time. That means the mere idea of bubbles will always be controversial, because no one wants to think they own an overvalued asset. In hindsight we're more likely to point cynical fingers than to learn lessons.

I don't think we'll ever be able to fully explain why bubbles occur. It's like asking why wars occur—there are almost always several reasons, many of them conflicting, all of them controversial.

It's too complicated a subject for simple answers.

But let me propose one reason they happen that both goes overlooked and applies to you personally: Investors often innocently take cues from other investors who are playing a different game than they are.

An idea exists in finance that seems innocent but has done incalculable damage.

It's the notion that assets have one rational price in a world where investors have different goals and time horizons.

Ask yourself: How much should you pay for Google stock today?

The answer depends on who "you" are.

Do you have a 30-year time horizon? Then the smart price to pay involves a sober analysis of Google's discounted cash flows over the next 30 years.

Are you looking to cash out within 10 years? Then the price to pay can be figured out by an analysis of the tech industry's potential over the next decade and whether Google management can execute on its vision.

Are you looking to sell within a year? Then pay attention to Google's current product sales cycles and whether we'll have a bear market.

Are you a day trader? Then the smart price to pay is "who cares?" because you're just trying to squeeze a few bucks out of whatever happens between now and lunchtime, which can be accomplished at any price.

When investors have different goals and time horizons—and they do in every asset class—prices that look ridiculous to one person can make sense to another, because the factors those investors pay attention to are different.

Take the dot-com bubble in the 1990s.

People can look at Yahoo! stock in 1999 and say "That was crazy! A zillion times revenue! The valuation made no sense!"

But many investors who owned Yahoo! stock in 1999 had time horizons so short that *it made sense for them* to pay a ridiculous price. A day trader could accomplish what they need whether Yahoo! was at $5 a share or $500 a share as long as it moved in the right direction that day. And it did, for years.

An iron rule of finance is that money chases returns to the greatest extent that it can. If an asset has momentum—it's been moving consistently up for a period of time—it's not crazy for a group of short-term traders to assume it will keep moving up. Not indefinitely; just for the short period of time they need it to. Momentum attracts short-term traders in a reasonable way.

Then it's off to the races.

Bubbles form when the momentum of short-term returns attracts enough money that the makeup of investors shifts from mostly long term to mostly short term.

That process feeds on itself. As traders push up short-term returns, they attract even more traders. Before long—and it often doesn't take long—the dominant market price-setters with the most authority are those with shorter time horizons.

Bubbles aren't so much about valuations rising. That's just a symptom of something else: time horizons shrinking as more short-term traders enter the playing field.

It's common to say the dot-com bubble was a time of irrational optimism about the future. But one of the most common headlines of that era was announcing record trading volume, which is what happens when investors are buying and selling in a *single day*. Investors—particularly the ones setting prices—were not thinking about the next 20 years. The average mutual fund had 120% annual turnover in 1999, meaning they were, at most, thinking about the next eight months. So were the individual investors who bought those mutual funds. Maggie Mahar wrote in her book *Bull!*:

> By the mid-nineties, the press had replaced annual scorecards with reports that appeared every three months. The change spurred investors to chase performance, rushing to buy the funds at the top of the charts, just when they were most expensive.

This was the era of day trading, short-term option contracts, and up-to-the minute market commentary. It's not the kind of thing you'd associate with long-term views.

The same thing happened during the housing bubble of the mid-2000s.

It's hard to justify paying $700,000 for a two-bedroom Florida track home to raise your family in for the next 10 years. But it makes perfect sense if you plan on flipping the home in a few months into a market with rising prices to make a quick profit. Which is exactly what many people were doing during the bubble.

Data from Attom, a company that tracks real estate transactions, shows the number of houses in America that sold more than once in a 12-month period—they were flipped—rose fivefold during the bubble, from 20,000 in the first quarter of 2000 to over 100,000 in the first quarter of 2004.[54] Flipping plunged after the bubble to less than 40,000 per quarter, where it's roughly remained since.

Do you think these flippers cared about long-term price-to-rent ratios? Or whether the prices they paid were backed up by long-term income growth? Of course not. Those numbers weren't relevant to their game. The only thing that mattered to flippers was that the price of the home would be more next month than it was this month. And for many years, it was.

You can say a lot about these investors. You can call them speculators. You can call them irresponsible. You can shake your head at their willingness to take huge risks.

But I don't think you can call all of them irrational.

The formation of bubbles isn't so much about people irrationally participating in long-term investing. They're about people somewhat rationally moving toward short-term trading to capture momentum that had been feeding on itself.

What do you expect people to do when momentum creates a big short-term return potential? Sit and watch patiently? Never. That's not how the world works. Profits will always be chased. And short-term traders operate in an area where the rules governing long-term investing—particularly around valuation—are ignored, because they're irrelevant to the game being played.

That's where things get interesting, and where the problems begin.

Bubbles do their damage when long-term investors playing one game start taking their cues from those short-term traders playing another.

Cisco stock rose 300% in 1999 to $60 per share. At that price the company was valued at $600 billion, which is insane. Few actually thought it was worth that much; the day-traders were just having their fun. Economist Burton Malkiel once pointed out that Cisco's implied growth rate at that valuation meant it would become larger than the entire U.S. economy within 20 years.

But if you were a long-term investor in 1999, $60 was the only price available to buy. And many people were buying it at that price. So you may have looked around and said to yourself, "Wow, maybe these other investors know something I don't." Maybe you went along with it. You even felt smart about it.

What you don't realize is that the traders who were setting

the marginal price of the stock were playing a different game than you were. Sixty dollars a share was a reasonable price for the traders, because they planned on selling the stock before the end of the day, when its price would probably be higher. But sixty dollars was a disaster in the making for you, because you planned on holding shares for the long run.

These two investors rarely even know that each other exist. But they're on the same field, running toward each other. When their paths blindly collide, someone gets hurt. Many finance and investment decisions are rooted in watching what other people do and either copying them or betting against them. But when you don't know why someone behaves like they do you won't know how long they'll continue acting that way, what will make them change their mind, or whether they'll ever learn their lesson.

When a commentator on CNBC says, "You should buy this stock," keep in mind that they do not know who you are. Are you a teenager trading for fun? An elderly widow on a limited budget? A hedge fund manager trying to shore up your books before the quarter ends? Are we supposed to think those three people have the same priorities, and that whatever level a particular stock is trading at is right for all three of them?

It's crazy.

It's hard to grasp that other investors have different goals than we do, because an anchor of psychology is not realizing that rational people can see the world through a different lens than your own. Rising prices persuade all investors in ways the best marketers envy. They are a drug that can turn value-conscious investors into dewy-eyed optimists, detached from their own reality by the actions of someone playing a different game than they are.

Being swayed by people playing a different game can also throw off how you think you're supposed to spend your money. So much consumer spending, particularly in developed countries, is socially driven: subtly influenced by people you admire, and done because you subtly want people to admire you.

But while we can see how much money other people spend on cars, homes, clothes, and vacations, we don't get to see their goals, worries, and aspirations. A young lawyer aiming to be a partner at a prestigious law firm might need to maintain an appearance that I, a writer who can work in sweatpants, have no need for. But when his purchases set my own expectations, I'm wandering down a path of potential disappointment because I'm spending the money without the career boost he's getting. We might not even have different styles. We're just playing a different game. It took me years to figure this out.

A takeaway here is that few things matter more with money than understanding your own time horizon and not being persuaded by the actions and behaviors of people playing different games than you are.

The main thing I can recommend is going out of your way to identify what game you're playing.

It's surprising how few of us do. We call everyone investing money "investors" like they're basketball players, all playing the same game with the same rules. When you realize how wrong that notion is you see how vital it is to simply identify what game you're playing. How I invest my own money is detailed in chapter 20, but years ago I wrote out "I am a passive investor optimistic in the world's ability to generate real economic growth and I'm confident that over the next 30 years that growth will accrue to my investments."

This might seem quaint, but once you write that mission statement down you realize everything that's unrelated to it—what the market did this year, or whether we'll have a recession next year—is part of a game I'm not playing. So I don't pay attention to it, and am in no danger of being persuaded by it.

Next, let's talk about pessimism.

17.

The Seduction of Pessimism

Optimism sounds like a sales pitch.
Pessimism sounds like someone trying to help you.

"For reasons I have never understood, people like to hear that the world is going to hell."

—Historian Deirdre McCloskey

OPTIMISM IS THE best bet for most people because the world tends to get better for most people most of the time.

But pessimism holds a special place in our hearts. Pessimism isn't just more common than optimism. It also sounds smarter. It's intellectually captivating, and it's paid more attention than optimism, which is often viewed as being oblivious to risk.

Before we go further we should define what optimism is. Real optimists don't believe that everything will be great. That's complacency. Optimism is a belief that the odds of a good outcome are in your favor over time, even when there will be setbacks along the way. The simple idea that most people wake up in the morning trying to make things a little better and more productive than wake up looking to cause trouble is the foundation of optimism. It's not complicated. It's not guaranteed, either. It's just the most reasonable bet for most people, most of the time. The late statistician Hans Rosling put it differently: "I am not an optimist. I am a very serious possibilist."

Now we can discuss optimism's more compelling sibling: pessimism.

December 29th, 2008.

The worst year for the economy in modern history is about to close. Stock markets around the world had collapsed. The global financial system was on day-to-day life support. Unemployment was surging.

As things looked like they couldn't get worse, *The Wall Street Journal* published a story arguing that we hadn't seen anything yet. It ran a front-page article on the outlook of a Russian professor named Igor Panarin whose economic views rival the flair of science fiction writers.

The *Journal* wrote:

> Around the end of June 2010, or early July, [Panarin] says, the U.S. will break into six pieces—with Alaska reverting to Russian control ... California will form the nucleus of what he calls "The Californian Republic," and will be part of China or under Chinese influence. Texas will be the heart of "The Texas Republic," a cluster of states that will go to Mexico or fall under Mexican influence. Washington, D.C., and New York will be part of an "Atlantic America" that may join the European Union. Canada will grab a group of Northern states Prof. Panarin calls "The Central North American Republic." Hawaii, he suggests, will be a protectorate of Japan or China, and Alaska will be subsumed into Russia.[55]

This was not the ramblings of a backroom blog or tinfoil-hat newsletter. This was on the front page of the most prestigious financial newspaper in the world.

It is fine to be pessimistic about the economy. It's even OK to be apocalyptic. History is full of examples of countries experiencing not just recessions, but disintegrations.

The interesting thing about Panarin-type stories is that their polar opposite—forecasts of outrageous optimism—are rarely taken as seriously as prophets of doom.

Take Japan in the late 1940s. The nation was gutted by defeat from World War II in every way—economically, industrially, culturally, socially. A brutal winter in 1946 caused a famine that limited food to less than 800 calories per person per day.[56]

Imagine if a Japanese academic had written a newspaper article during this time that said:

> Chin up, everyone. Within our lifetime our economy will grow to almost 15 times the size it was before the end of the war. Our life expectancy will nearly double. Our stock market will produce returns like any country in history has rarely seen. We will go more than 40 years without ever seeing unemployment top 6%. We will become a world leader in electronic innovation and corporate managerial systems. Before long we will be so rich that we will own some of the most prized real estate in the United States. Americans, by the way, will be our closest ally and will try to copy our economic insights.

They would have been summarily laughed out of the room and asked to seek a medical evaluation.

Keep in mind the description above is *what actually happened* in Japan in the generation after the war. But the mirror opposite of Panarin looks absurd in a way a forecast of doom doesn't.

Pessimism just sounds smarter and more plausible than optimism.

Tell someone that everything will be great and they're likely to either shrug you off or offer a skeptical eye. Tell someone they're in danger and you have their undivided attention.

If a smart person tells me they have a stock pick that's going to rise 10-fold in the next year, I will immediately write them off as full of nonsense.

If someone who's full of nonsense tells me that a stock I own is about to collapse because it's an accounting fraud, I will clear my calendar and listen to their every word.

Say we'll have a big recession and newspapers will call you. Say we're headed for average growth and no one particularly cares. Say we're nearing the next Great Depression and you'll get on TV. But mention that good times are ahead, or markets have room to run, or that a company has huge potential, and a common reaction from commentators and spectators alike is that you are either a salesman or comically aloof of risks.

The investing newsletter industry has known this for years, and is now populated by prophets of doom despite operating in an environment where the stock market has gone up 17,000-fold in the last century (including dividends).

This is true beyond finance. Matt Ridley wrote in his book *The Rational Optimist*:

> A constant drumbeat of pessimism usually drowns out any triumphalist song ... If you say the world has been getting better you may get away with being called naïve and insensitive. If you say the world is going to go on getting better, you are considered embarrassingly mad. If, on the other hand, you say catastrophe is imminent, you may expect a McArthur genius award or even the Nobel Peace Prize. In my own adult lifetime ... the fashionable reasons for pessimism changed, but the pessimism was constant.

"Every group of people I ask thinks the world is more frightening, more violent, and more hopeless—in short, more dramatic—than it really is," Hans Rosling wrote in his book *Factfulness*.

When you realize how much progress humans can make during a lifetime in everything from economic growth to medical breakthroughs to stock market gains to social equality, you would think optimism would gain more attention than pessimism. And yet.

The intellectual allure of pessimism has been known for ages. John Stuart Mill wrote in the 1840s: "I have observed that not the man who hopes when others despair, but the man who despairs when others hope, is admired by a large class of persons as a sage."

The question is, why? And how does it impact how we think about money?

Let's repeat the premise that no one is crazy.

There are valid reasons why pessimism is seductive when dealing with money. It just helps to know what they are to ensure we don't take them too far.

Part of it is instinctual and unavoidable. Kahneman says the asymmetric aversion to loss is an evolutionary shield. He writes:

> When directly compared or weighted against each other, losses loom larger than gains. This asymmetry between the power of positive and negative expectations or experiences has an evolutionary history. Organisms that treat threats as more urgent than opportunities have a better chance to survive and reproduce.

But a few other things make financial pessimism easy, common, and more persuasive than optimism.

One is that money is ubiquitous, so something bad happening tends to affect everyone and captures everyone's attention.

That isn't true of, say, weather. A hurricane barreling down on Florida poses no direct risk to 92% of Americans. But a recession barreling down on the economy could impact every single person—including you, *so pay attention.*

This goes for something as specific as the stock market. More than half of all American households directly own stocks.[57] Even among those that don't, the stock market's gyrations are promoted so heavily in the media that the Dow Jones Industrial Average might be the stock-less household's most-watched economic barometer.

Stocks rising 1% might be briefly mentioned in the evening news. But a 1% fall will be reported in bold, all-caps letters usually written in blood red. The asymmetry is hard to avoid.

And while few question or try to explain why the market went up—isn't it supposed to go up?—there is almost always an attempt to explain why it went down.

Are investors worried about economic growth?

Did the Fed screw things up again?

Are politicians making bad decisions?

Is there another shoe to drop?

Narratives about why a decline occurred make them easier to talk about, worry about, and frame a story around what you think will happen next—usually, more of the same.

Even if you don't own stocks, those kind of things will grab your attention. Only 2.5% of Americans owned stocks on the eve of the great crash of 1929 that sparked the Great Depression. But the majority of Americans—if not the world—watched in amazement as the market collapsed, wondering what it signaled about their own fate. This was true whether you were a lawyer or a farmer or a car mechanic.

Historian Eric Rauchway writes:

> This fall in value immediately afflicted only a few Americans. But so closely had the others watched the market and regarded it as an index of their fates that they suddenly stopped much of their economic activity. As the economist Joseph Schumpeter later wrote, "people felt that the ground under their feet was giving way."[58]

There are two topics that will affect your life whether you are interested in them or not: money and health. While health issues tend to be individual, money issues are more systemic. In a connected system where one person's decisions can affect everyone else, it's understandable why financial risks gain a spotlight and capture attention in a way few other topics can.

Another is that pessimists often extrapolate present trends without accounting for how markets adapt.

In 2008 environmentalist Lester Brown wrote: "By 2030 China would need 98 million barrels of oil a day. The world is currently producing 85 million barrels a day and may never produce much more than that. There go the world's oil reserves."[59]

He's right. The world would run out of oil in that scenario.

But that's not how markets work.

There is an iron law in economics: extremely good and extremely bad circumstances rarely stay that way for long because supply and demand adapt in hard-to-predict ways.

Consider what happened to oil immediately after Brown's prediction.

Oil prices surged in 2008 as growing global demand—much of it from China—crept up to potential output. A barrel of oil sold for $20 in 2001 and $138 by 2008.[60]

The new price meant drilling oil was like pulling gold out of the ground. The incentives for oil producers changed dramatically. Hard-to-tap oil supplies that weren't worth the fight at $20 a barrel—the cost of drilling didn't offset the price you could sell it for—became the bonanza of a lifetime now that you could sell a barrel for $138.

That sparked a surge of new fracking and horizontal drilling technologies.

The Earth has had roughly the same amount of oil reserves for all of human history. And we've known where the big oil deposits are for some time. What changes is the technology we have that lets us economically pull the stuff out of the ground. Oil historian Daniel Yergin writes: "86% of oil reserves in the United States are the result not of what is estimated at time of discovery but of the revisions" that come when our technology improves.

That's what happened as fracking took off in 2008. In the United States alone oil production went from roughly five million barrels per day in 2008 to 13 million by 2019.[61] World oil production is now over 100 million barrels per day—some 20% above what Brown assumed was the high mark.

To a pessimist extrapolating oil trends in 2008, of course things looked bad. To a realist who understood that necessity is the mother of all invention, it was far less scary.

Assuming that something ugly will stay ugly is an easy forecast to make. And it's persuasive, because it doesn't require imagining the world changing. But problems correct and people adapt. Threats incentivize solutions in equal magnitude. That's a common plot of economic history that is too easily forgotten by pessimists who forecast in straight lines.

A third is that progress happens too slowly to notice, but setbacks happen too quickly to ignore.

There are lots of overnight tragedies. There are rarely overnight miracles.

On January 5th, 1889, the *Detroit Free Press* pushed back against the long-held dream that man could one day fly like a bird. Airplanes, the paper wrote, "appear impossible":

> The smallest possible weight of a flying machine, with the necessary fuel and engineer, could not be less than 300 or 400 pounds ... but there is a low limit of weight, certainly not much beyond fifty pounds, beyond which it is impossible for

> an animal to fly. Nature has reached this limit, and with her utmost effort has failed to pass it.

Six months later, Orville Wright dropped out of high school to help his brother, Wilbur, tinker in their backyard shed to build a printing press. It was the brothers' first joint invention. It would not be their last.

If you had to make a list of the most important inventions of the 20th century, the airplane would be at least top five, if not number one. The airplane changed *everything*. It started world wars, it ended world wars. It connected the world, bridging gaps between cities and rural communities; oceans and countries.

But the story of the Wright Brothers' quest to build the first plane has a fascinating twist.

After they conquered flight, no one seemed to notice. Nobody seemed to care.

In his 1952 book on American history, Frederick Lewis Allen wrote:

> Several years went by before the public grasped what the Wrights were doing; people were so convinced that flying was impossible that most of those who saw them flying about Dayton [Ohio] in 1905 decided that what they had seen must be some trick without significance—somewhat as most people today would regard a demonstration of, say, telepathy. It was not until May, 1908—nearly four and a half years after the Wright's first flight—that experienced reporters were sent to observe what they were doing, experienced editors gave full credence to these reporters' excited dispatches, and the world at last woke up to the fact that human flight had been successfully accomplished.

Even after people caught on to the plane's wonder, they underestimated it for years.

First it was seen mainly as a military weapon. Then a rich person's toy. Then, perhaps, used to transport a few people.

The Washington Post wrote in 1909: "There will never be such a thing as commercial aerial freighters. Freight will continue to drag its slow weight across the patient earth." The first cargo plane took off five months later.

Now compare that slow, years-long awakening to becoming optimistic about the airplane to how quickly people pay attention to drivers of pessimism, like a corporate bankruptcy.

Or a major war.

Or a plane *crash*. Some of the first mentions of the Wright's plane came in 1908 when an Army Lieutenant named Thomas Selfridge was killed during a demonstration flight.[62]

Growth is driven by compounding, which always takes time. Destruction is driven by single points of failure, which can happen in seconds, and loss of confidence, which can happen in an instant.

It's easier to create a narrative around pessimism because the story pieces tend to be fresher and more recent. Optimistic narratives require looking at a long stretch of history and developments, which people tend to forget and take more effort to piece together.

Consider the progress of medicine. Looking at the last year will do you little good. Any single decade won't do much better. But looking at the last 50 years will show something extraordinary. For example, the age-adjusted death rate per capita from heart disease has declined more than 70% since 1965, according to the National Institute of Health.[63] A 70% decline in heart-disease death is enough to save something like half a million American lives per year. Picture the population of Atlanta *saved every year*. But since that progress happened so slowly, it captures less attention than quick, sudden losses like terrorism, plane crashes, or natural disasters. We could have a Hurricane Katrina five times a week, every week—imagine how much attention that would receive—and it would not offset the number of annual lives saved by the decline in heart disease in the last 50 years.

This same thing applies to business, where it takes years to realize how important a product or company is, but failures can happen overnight.

And in stock markets, where a 40% decline that takes place in six months will draw congressional investigations, but a 140% gain that takes place over six years can go virtually unnoticed.

And in careers, where reputations take a lifetime to build and a single email to destroy.

The short sting of pessimism prevails while the powerful pull of optimism goes unnoticed.

This underscores an important point made previously in this book: In investing you must identify the price of success—volatility and loss amid the long backdrop of growth—and be willing to pay it.

In 2004 *The New York Times* interviewed Stephen Hawking, the scientist whose incurable motor-neuron disease left him paralyzed and unable to talk at age 21.

Through his computer, Hawking told the interviewer how excited he was to sell books to lay people.

"Are you always this cheerful?" the *Times* asked.

"My expectations were reduced to zero when I was 21. Everything since then has been a bonus," he replied.

Expecting things to be great means a best-case scenario that feels flat. Pessimism reduces expectations, narrowing the gap between possible outcomes and outcomes you feel great about.

Maybe that's why it's so seductive. Expecting things to be bad is the best way to be pleasantly surprised when they're not.

Which, ironically, is something to be optimistic about.

Now, a short story about stories.

18.

When You'll Believe Anything

Appealing fictions, and why stories are more powerful than statistics.

IMAGINE AN ALIEN dispatched to Earth. His job is to keep tabs on our economy.

He circles above New York City, trying to size up the economy and how it changed between 2007 and 2009.

On New Year's Eve 2007 he hovers over Times Square. He sees tens of thousands of happy partygoers surrounded by bright lights, monstrous billboards, fireworks, and TV cameras.

He comes back to Times Square on New Year's Eve 2009. He sees tens of thousands of happy partygoers surrounded by bright lights, monstrous billboards, fireworks, and TV cameras.

It looks about the same. He cannot see much difference.

He sees roughly the same number of New Yorkers hustling around the city. Those people are surrounded by the same number of office buildings, which house the same number of desks with the same number of computers, hooked up to the same number of internet connections.

Outside the city he sees the same number of factories and warehouses, connected by the same highways, carrying the same number of trucks.

He gets a little closer to the ground and sees the same universities teaching the same topics and handing out the same degrees to the same number of people.

He sees the same number of patents protecting the same groundbreaking ideas.

He notices that technology has improved. Everyone in 2009

carries smartphones that didn't exist in 2007. Computers are now faster. Medicine is better. Cars get better gas mileage. Solar and fracking technology has advanced. Social media has grown exponentially.

As he flies around the country he sees the same. Around the globe, more of the same.

The economy is in about the same shape, maybe even better, in 2009 as it was in 2007, he concludes.

Then he looks at the numbers.

He's shocked that U.S. households are $16 trillion poorer in 2009 than they were in 2007.

He's dumbfounded that 10 million more Americans are unemployed.

He's in disbelief when he learns the stock market is worth half of what it was two years before.

He can't believe that people's forecast of their economic potential has plunged.

"I don't get it," he says. "I've seen the cities. I've looked at the factories. You guys have the same knowledge, the same tools, the same ideas. Nothing has changed! Why are you poorer? Why are you more pessimistic?"

There was one change the alien couldn't see between 2007 and 2009: The stories we told ourselves about the economy.

In 2007, we told a story about the stability of housing prices, the prudence of bankers, and the ability of financial markets to accurately price risk.

In 2009 we stopped believing that story.

That's the only thing that changed. But it made all the difference in the world.

Once the narrative that home prices will keep rising broke, mortgage defaults rose, then banks lost money, then they reduced lending to other businesses, which led to layoffs, which led to less spending, which led to more layoffs, and on and on.

Other than clinging to a new narrative, we had an identical—if not greater—capacity for wealth and growth in 2009 as we did in 2007. Yet the economy suffered its worst hit in 80 years.

This is different from, say, Germany in 1945, whose manufacturing base had been obliterated. Or Japan in the 2000s, whose working-age population was shrinking. That's *tangible* economic damage. In 2009 we inflicted *narrative* damage on ourselves, and it was vicious. It's one of the most potent economic forces that exists.

When we think about the growth of economies, businesses, investments and careers, we tend to think about tangible things—how much stuff do we have and what are we capable of?

But stories are, by far, the most powerful force in the economy. They are the fuel that can let the tangible parts of the economy work, or the brake that holds our capabilities back.

At the personal level, there are two things to keep in mind about a story-driven world when managing your money.

---

1. The more you want something to be true, the more likely you are to believe a story that overestimates the odds of it being true.

What was the happiest day of your life?

The documentary *How to Live Forever* asks that innocent question to a centenarian who offered an amazing response.

"Armistice Day," she said, referring to the 1918 agreement that ended World War I.

"Why?" the producer asks.

"Because we knew there would be no more wars ever again," she says.

World War II began 21 years later, killing 75 million people.

There are many things in life that we think are true because we desperately want them to be true.

I call these things "appealing fictions." They have a big impact on how we think about money—particularly investments and the economy.

An appealing fiction happens when you are smart, you want to find solutions, but face a combination of limited control and high stakes.

They are extremely powerful. They can make you believe just about anything.

Take a short example.

Ali Hajaji's son was sick. Elders in his Yemeni village proposed a folk remedy: shove the tip of a burning stick through his son's chest to drain the sickness from his body.

After the procedure, Hajaji told *The New York Times*: "When you have no money, and your son is sick, you'll believe anything."[64]

Medicine predates useful medicine by thousands of years. Before the scientific method and the discovery of germs there was blood-letting, starvation therapy, cutting holes in your body to let the evils out, and other treatments that did nothing but hasten your demise.

It seems crazy. But if you desperately need a solution and a good one isn't known or readily available to you, the path of least resistance is toward Hajaji's reasoning: willing to believe anything. Not just try anything, but believe it.

Chronicling the Great Plague of London, Daniel Defoe wrote in 1722:

> The people were more addicted to prophecies and astrological conjurations, dreams, and old wives' tales than ever they were before or since ... almanacs frighted them terribly ... the posts of houses and corners of streets were plastered over with doctors' bills and papers of ignorant fellows, quacking and inviting the

> people to come to them for remedies, which was generally set off with such flourishes as these: 'Infallible preventive pills against the plague.' 'Neverfailing preservatives against the infection.' 'Sovereign cordials against the corruption of the air.'

The plague killed a quarter of Londoners in 18 months. You'll believe just about anything when the stakes are that high.

Now think about how the same set of limited information and high stakes impact our financial decisions.

Why do people listen to TV investment commentary that has little track record of success? Partly because the stakes are so high in investing. Get a few stock picks right and you can become rich without much effort. If there's a 1% chance that someone's prediction will come true, and it coming true will change your life, it's not crazy to pay attention—just in case.

And there are so many financial opinions that once you pick a strategy or side, you become invested in them both financially and mentally. If you want a certain stock to rise 10-fold, that's your tribe. If you think a certain economic policy will spark hyperinflation, that's your side.

These may be low-probability bets. The problem is that viewers can't, or don't, calibrate low odds, like a 1% chance. Many default to a firm belief that what they want to be true is unequivocally true. But they're only doing that because the possibility of a huge outcome exists.

Investing is one of the only fields that offers daily opportunities for extreme rewards. People believe in financial quackery in a way they never would for, say, weather quackery because the rewards for correctly predicting what the stock market will do next week are in a different universe than the rewards for predicting whether it will be sunny or rainy next week.

Consider that 85% of active mutual funds underperformed their benchmark over the 10 years ending 2018.[65] That figure has been fairly stable for generations. You would think an industry with such poor performance would be a niche service and have a hard time staying in business. But there's almost five trillion dollars invested in these funds.[66] Give someone the chance of investing alongside "the next Warren Buffett" and they'll believe with such faith that millions of people will put their life savings behind it.

Or take Bernie Madoff. In hindsight his Ponzi scheme should have been obvious. He reported returns that never varied, they were audited by a relatively unknown accounting firm, and he refused to release much information on how the returns were achieved. Yet Madoff raised billions of dollars from some of the most sophisticated investors in the world. He told a good story, and people wanted to believe it.

This is a big part of why room for error, flexibility, and financial independence—important themes discussed in previous chapters—are indispensable.

The bigger the gap between what you want to be true and what you need to be true to have an acceptable outcome, the more you are protecting yourself from falling victim to an appealing financial fiction.

When thinking about room for error in a forecast it is tempting to think that potential outcomes range from you being just right enough to you being very, very right. But the biggest risk is that you want something to be true so badly that the range of your forecast isn't even in the same ballpark as reality.

In its last 2007 meeting the Federal Reserve predicted what economic growth would be in 2008 and 2009.[67] Already weary of a weakening economy, it was not optimistic. It predicted a range of potential growth—1.6% growth on the low end, 2.8% on the high end. That was its margin of safety, its room for error. In reality the economy contracted by more than 2%, meaning the Fed's low-end estimate was off by almost threefold.

It's hard for a policymaker to predict an outright recession, because a recession will make their careers complicated. So even worst-case projections rarely expect anything worse than just "slow-ish" growth. It's an appealing fiction, and it's easy to believe because expecting anything worse is too painful to consider.

Policymakers are easy targets for criticism, but all of us do this to some extent. And we do it in both directions. If you think a recession is coming and you cash out your stocks in anticipation, your view of the economy is suddenly going to be warped by what you want to happen. Every blip, every anecdote, will look like a sign that doom has arrived—maybe not because it has, but because you want it to.

Incentives are a powerful motivator, and we should always remember how they influence our own financial goals and outlooks. It can't be overstated: there is no greater force in finance than room for error, and the higher the stakes, the wider it should be.

2. Everyone has an incomplete view of the world. But we form a complete narrative to fill in the gaps.

My daughter is about a year old as I write this. She's curious about everything and learns so fast.

But sometimes I think about all the stuff she can't comprehend.

She has no idea why her dad goes to work every morning.

The concept of bills, budgets, careers, promotions, and saving for retirement are completely foreign to her.

Imagine trying to explain the Federal Reserve, credit derivatives, or NAFTA to her. Impossible.

But her world isn't dark. She does not wander around in confusion.

Even at a year old, she's written her own internal narrative of how everything works. Blankets keep you warm, mom snuggles keep you safe, and dates taste good.

Everything she comes across fits into one of a few dozen mental models she's learned. When I go to work she doesn't stop in confusion, wondering what salary and bills are. She has a crystal clear explanation of the situation: Dad isn't playing with me, and I wanted him to play with me, so I'm sad.

Even though she knows little, she doesn't realize it, because she tells herself a coherent story about what's going on based on the little she does know.

All of us, no matter our age, do the same thing.

Just like my daughter, I don't know what I don't know. So I am just as susceptible to explaining the world through the limited set of mental models I have at my disposal.

Like her, I look for the most understandable causes in everything I come across. And, like her, I'm wrong about a lot of them, because I know a lot less about how the world works than I think I do.

This is true for the most fact-based of subjects.

Take history. It's just the recounting of stuff that already happened. It should be clear and objective. But as B. H. Liddell Hart writes in the book *Why Don't We Learn From History?*:

> [History] cannot be interpreted without the aid of imagination and intuition. The sheer quantity of evidence is so overwhelming that selection is inevitable. Where there is selection there is art. Those who read history tend to look for what proves them right and confirms their personal opinions. They defend loyalties. They read with a purpose to affirm or to attack. They resist inconvenient truth since everyone wants to be on the side of the angels. Just as we start wars to end all wars.

Daniel Kahneman once told me about the stories people tell themselves to make sense of the past. He said:

> Hindsight, the ability to explain the past, gives us the illusion

> that the world is understandable. It gives us the illusion that the world makes sense, even when it doesn't make sense. That's a big deal in producing mistakes in many fields.

Most people, when confronted with something they don't understand, do not realize they don't understand it because they're able to come up with an explanation that makes sense based on their own unique perspective and experiences in the world, however limited those experiences are. We all want the complicated world we live in to make sense. So we tell ourselves stories to fill in the gaps of what are effectively blind spots.

What these stories do to us financially can be both fascinating and terrifying.

When I'm blind to parts of how the world works I might completely misunderstand why the stock market is behaving like it is, in a way that gives me too much confidence in my ability to know what it might do next. Part of the reason forecasting the stock market and the economy is so hard is because you are the only person in the world who thinks the world operates the way you do. When you make decisions for reasons that I can't even comprehend, I might follow you blindly into a decision that's right for you and disastrous to me. This, as we saw in chapter 16, is how bubbles form.

Coming to terms with how much you don't know means coming to terms with how much of what happens in the world is out of your control. And that can be hard to accept.

Think about market forecasts. We're very, very bad at them. I once calculated that if you just assume that the market goes up every year by its historic average, your accuracy is better than if you follow the average annual forecasts of the top 20 market strategists from large Wall Street banks. Our ability to predict recessions isn't much better. And since big events come out of nowhere, forecasts may do more harm than good, giving the illusion of predictability in a world where unforeseen events control most outcomes. Carl Richards writes: "Risk is what's left over when you think you've thought of everything."

People know this. I have not met an investor who genuinely thinks market forecasts as a whole are accurate or useful. But there's still tremendous demand for forecasts, in both the media and from financial advisors.

Why?

Psychologist Philip Tetlock once wrote: "We need to believe we live in a predictable, controllable world, so we turn to authoritative-sounding people who promise to satisfy that need."

Satisfying that need is a great way to put it. Wanting to believe we are in control is an emotional itch that needs to be scratched, rather than an analytical problem to be calculated and solved. The illusion of control is more persuasive than the reality of uncertainty. So we cling to stories about outcomes being in our control.

Part of this has to do with confusing fields of precision with fields of uncertainty.

NASA's New Horizons spacecraft passed by Pluto two years ago. It was a three-billion mile trip that took nine and a half years. According to NASA, the trip "took about one minute less than predicted when the craft was launched in January 2006."[68]

Think about that. In an untested, decade-long journey, NASA's forecast was 99.99998% accurate. That's like forecasting a trip from New York to Boston and being accurate to within four millionths of a second.

But astrophysics is a field of precession. It isn't impacted by the vagaries of human behavior and emotions, like finance is. Business, economics, and investing, are fields of uncertainty, overwhelmingly driven by decisions that can't easily be explained with clean formulas, like a trip to Pluto can. But we desperately want it to be like a trip to Pluto, because the idea of a NASA engineer being in 99.99998% control of an outcome is beautiful and comforting. It's so comforting that we're tempted to tell ourselves stories about how much control we have in other parts of our life, like money.

Kahneman once laid out the path these stories take:

- When planning we focus on what we want to do and can do, neglecting the plans and skills of others whose decisions might affect our outcomes.
- Both in explaining the past and in predicting the future, we focus on the causal role of skill and neglect the role of luck.
- We focus on what we know and neglect what we do not know, which makes us overly confident in our beliefs.

He described how this impacts businesses:

> I have had several occasions to ask founders and participants in innovative start-ups a question: To what extent will the outcome of your effort depend on what you do in your firm? This is evidently an easy question; the answer comes quickly and it has never been less than 80%. Even when they are not sure they will succeed, these bold people think their fate is almost entirely in their own hands. They are surely wrong: the outcome of a start-up depends as much on the achievements of its competitors and on changes in the market as on its own efforts. However, entrepreneurs naturally focus on what they know best—their plans and actions and the most immediate threats and opportunities, such as the availability of funding. They know less about their competitors and therefore find it natural to imagine a future in which the competition plays little part.

We all do this to some extent.

And like my daughter, it doesn't bother us a bit.

We don't wander around blind and confused. We have to think the world we operate in makes sense based on what we happen to know. It'd be too hard to get out of bed in the morning if you felt otherwise.

But the alien circling over Earth?

The one who's confident he knows what's happening based on what he sees but turns out to be completely wrong because he can't know the stories going on inside everyone else's head?

He's all of us.

19.

All Together Now

What we've learned about the psychology of your own money.

CONGRATULATIONS, YOU'RE STILL reading.

It's time to tie together a few things we've learned.

This chapter is a bit of a summary; a few short and actionable lessons that can help you make better financial decisions.

First, let me tell you a story about a dentist appointment gone horribly awry. It teaches us something vital about the dangers of giving advice about what to do with your money.

Clarence Hughes went to the dentist in 1931. His mouth was radiating pain. His dentist put him under crude anesthesia to ease the pain. When Clarence awoke hours later he had 16 fewer teeth and his tonsils removed.

And then everything went wrong. Clarence died a week later from his surgery's complications.

His wife sued the dentist, but not because the surgery went awry. Every surgery risked death in 1931.

Clarence, she said, never consented to the procedures in the first place, and wouldn't if he were asked.

The case wove through courts, but went nowhere. Consent between doctor and patient wasn't black and white in 1931. One court summed up the idea that doctors require freedom to make the best medical decisions: "Without such, we could not enjoy the advancement of science."

For most of history the ethos of medicine was that the doctor's job was to fix the patient, and what the patient thought about the doctor's treatment plans wasn't relevant. Dr. Jay Katz wrote about the philosophy in his book *The Silent World Between Doctor and Patient*:

> Doctors felt that in order to accomplish that objective they were obligated to attend to their patients' physical and emotional needs and to do so on their own authority, without consulting with their patients about the decisions that needed to be made. The idea that patients may also be entitled to sharing the burdens of decisions with their doctors was never part of the ethos of medicine.

This wasn't ego or malice. It was a belief in two points:

1. Every patient wants to be cured.
2. There is a universal and right way to cure them.

Not requiring patient consent in treatment plans makes sense if you believe in those two points.

But that's not how medicine works.

In the last 50 years medical schools subtly shifted teaching away from treating disease and toward treating patients. That meant laying out the options of treatment plans, and then letting the patient decide the best path forward.

This trend was partly driven by patient-protection laws, partly by Katz's influential book, which argued that patients have wildly different views about what's worth it in medicine, so their beliefs have to be taken into consideration. Katz wrote:

> It is dangerous nonsense to assert that in the practice of their art and science physicians can rely on their benevolent intentions, their abilities to judge what is the right thing to do ... It is not that easy. Medicine is a complex profession and the interactions between physicians and patients are also complex.

That last line is important. "Medicine is a complex profession and the interactions between physicians and patients are also complex."

You know what profession is the same? Financial advice.

I can't tell you what to do with your money, because I don't know you.

I don't know what you want. I don't know when you want it. I don't why you want it.

So I'm not going to tell you what to do with your money. I don't want to treat you like a dentist treated Clarence Hughes.

But doctors and dentists aren't useless, obviously. They have knowledge. They know the odds. They know what tends to work, even if patients come to different conclusions about what kind of treatment is right for them.

Financial advisors are the same. There are universal truths in money, even if people come to different conclusions about how they want to apply those truths to their own finances.

With that caveat in place, let's look at a few short recommendations that can help you make better decisions with your money.

Go out of your way to find humility when things are going right and forgiveness/compassion when they go wrong. Because it's never as good or as bad as it looks. The world is big and complex. Luck and risk are both real and hard to identify. Do so when judging both yourself and others. Respect the power of luck and risk and you'll have a better chance of focusing on things you can actually control. You'll also have a better chance of finding the right role models.

Less ego, more wealth. Saving money is the gap between your ego and your income, and wealth is what you don't see. So wealth is created by suppressing what you could buy today in order to have more stuff or more options in the future. No matter how much you earn, you will never build wealth unless you can put a lid on how much fun you can have with your money right now, today.

Manage your money in a way that helps you sleep at night. That's different from saying you should aim to earn the highest returns or save a specific percentage of your income. Some people won't sleep well unless they're earning the highest returns; others will only get a good rest if they're conservatively invested. To each their own. But the foundation of, "does this help me sleep at night?" is the best universal guidepost for all financial decisions.

If you want to do better as an investor, the single most powerful thing you can do is increase your time horizon. Time is the most powerful force in investing. It makes little things grow big and big mistakes fade away. It can't neutralize luck and risk, but it pushes results closer towards what people deserve.

Become OK with a lot of things going wrong. You can be wrong half the time and still make a fortune, because a small minority of things account for the majority of outcomes. No matter what you're doing with your money you should be comfortable with a lot of stuff not working. That's just how the world is. So you should always measure how you've done by looking at your full portfolio, rather than individual investments. It is fine to have a large chunk of poor investments and a few outstanding ones. That's usually the best-case scenario. Judging how you've done by focusing on individual investments makes winners look more brilliant than they were, and losers appear more regrettable than they should.

Use money to gain control over your time, because not having control of your time is such a powerful and universal drag on happiness. The ability to do what you want, when you want, with who you want, for as long as you want to, pays the highest dividend that exists in finance.

Be nicer and less flashy. No one is impressed with your possessions as much as you are. You might think you want a fancy car or a nice watch. But what you probably want is respect and admiration. And you're more likely to gain those things through kindness and humility than horsepower and chrome.

Save. Just save. You don't need a specific reason to save. It's great to save for a car, or a downpayment, or a medical emergency. But saving for things that are impossible to predict or define is one of the best reasons to save. Everyone's life is a continuous chain of surprises. Savings that aren't earmarked for anything in particular is a hedge against life's inevitable ability to surprise the hell out of you at the worst possible moment.

Define the cost of success and be ready to pay it. Because nothing worthwhile is free. And remember that most financial costs don't have visible price tags. Uncertainty, doubt, and regret are common costs in the finance world. They're often worth paying. But you have to view them as fees (a price worth paying to get something nice in exchange) rather than fines (a penalty you should avoid).

Worship room for error. A gap between what could happen in the future and what you need to happen in the future in order to do well is what gives you endurance, and endurance is what makes compounding magic over time. Room for error often looks like a conservative hedge, but if it keeps you in the game it can pay for itself many times over.

Avoid the extreme ends of financial decisions. Everyone's goals and desires will change over time, and the more extreme your past decisions were the more you may regret them as you evolve.

You should like risk because it pays off over time. But you should be paranoid of ruinous risk because it prevents you from taking future risks that will pay off over time.

Define the game you're playing, and make sure your actions are not being influenced by people playing a different game.

Respect the mess. Smart, informed, and reasonable people can disagree in finance, because people have vastly different goals and desires. There is no single right answer; just the answer that works for you.

Now let me tell you what works for me.

20.

Confessions

The psychology of my own money.

SANDY GOTTESMAN, A billionaire investor who founded the consulting group First Manhattan, is said to ask one question when interviewing candidates for his investment team: "What do you own, and why?"

Not, "What stocks do you think are cheap?" or "What economy is about to have a recession?"

Just show me what you do with your own money.

I love this question because it highlights what can often be a mile-wide gap between what makes sense—which is what people suggest you do—and what feels right to them—which is what they actually do.

Half of all U.S. mutual fund portfolio managers do not invest a cent of their own money in their funds, according to Morningstar.[69] This might seem atrocious, and surely the statistic uncovers some hypocrisy.

But this kind of stuff is more common than you'd think. Ken Murray, a professor of medicine at USC, wrote an essay in 2011 titled "How Doctors Die" that showed the degree to which doctors choose different end-of-life treatments for themselves than they recommend for their patients.[70]

"[Doctors] don't die like the rest of us," he wrote. "What's unusual about them is not how much treatment they get compared to most Americans, but how little. For all the time they spend fending off the deaths of others, they tend to be fairly serene when faced with death themselves. They know exactly what is going to happen, they know the choices, and they generally have access to any sort of medical care they could want. But they go gently." A doctor may throw the kitchen sink at her patient's cancer, but choose palliative care for herself.

The difference between what someone suggests you do and what they do for themselves isn't always a bad thing. It just underscores that when dealing with complicated and emotional issues that affect you and your family, there is no one right answer. There is no universal truth. There's only what works for you and your family, checking the boxes you want checked in a way that leaves you comfortable and sleeping well at night.

There are basic principles that must be adhered to—this is true in finance and in medicine—but important financial decisions are not made in spreadsheets or in textbooks. They are made at the dinner table. They often aren't made with the intention of maximizing returns, but minimizing the chance of disappointing a spouse or child. Those kinds of things are difficult to summarize in charts or formulas, and they vary widely from person to person. What works for one person may not work for another.

You have to find what works for you. Here's what works for me.

How my family thinks about savings

Charlie Munger once said "I did not intend to get rich. I just wanted to get independent."

We can leave aside rich, but independence has always been my personal financial goal. Chasing the highest returns or leveraging my assets to live the most luxurious life has little interest to me. Both look like games people do to impress their friends, and both have hidden risks. I mostly just want to wake up every day knowing my family and I can do whatever we want to do on our own terms. Every financial decision we make revolves around that goal.

My parents lived their adult years in two stages: dirt poor and moderately well off. My father became a doctor when he was 40 and already had three kids. Earning a doctor's salary did not offset the frugal mentality that is forced when supporting three hungry kids while in medical school, and my parents spent the good years living well below their means with a high savings rate. This gave them a degree of independence. My father was an Emergency Room doctor, one of the highest-stress professions I can imagine and one that requires a painful toggling of circadian rhythms between night and day shifts. After two decades he decided he'd had enough, so he stopped. Just quit. Moved onto the next phase of his life.

That stuck with me. Being able to wake up one morning and change what you're doing, on your own terms, whenever you're ready, seems like the grandmother of all financial goals. Independence, to me, doesn't mean you'll stop working. It means you only do the work you like with people you like at the times you want for as long as you want.

And achieving some level of independence does not rely on earning a doctor's income. It's mostly a matter of keeping your expectations in check and living below your means. Independence, at any income level, is driven by your savings rate. And past a certain level of income your savings rate is driven by your ability to keep your lifestyle expectations from running away.

My wife and I met in college and moved in with each other years before we got married. After school we both had entry-level jobs with entry-level pay, and settled into a moderate lifestyle. All lifestyles exist on a spectrum, and what is decent to one person can feel like royalty or poverty to another. But at our incomes we got what we considered a decent apartment, a decent car, decent clothes, decent food. Comfortable, but nothing close to fancy.

Despite more than a decade of rising incomes—myself in finance, my wife in health care—we've more or less stayed at that lifestyle ever since. That's pushed our savings rate continuously higher. Virtually every dollar of raise has accrued to savings—our "independence fund." We now live considerably below our means, which tells you little about our income and more about our decision to maintain a lifestyle that we established in our 20s.

If there's a part of our household financial plan I'm proud of it's that we got the goalpost of lifestyle desires to stop moving at a young age. Our savings rate is fairly high, but we rarely feel like we're repressively frugal because our aspirations for more stuff haven't moved much. It's not that our aspirations are nonexistent—we like nice stuff and live comfortably. We just got the goalpost to stop moving.

This would not work for everyone, and it only works for us because we both agree to it equally—neither of us are compromising for the other. Most of what we get pleasure from—going for walks, reading, podcasts—costs little, so we rarely feel like we're missing out. On the rare occasion when I question our savings rate I think of the independence my parents earned from years of high savings, and I quickly come back. Independence is our top goal. A secondary benefit of maintaining a lifestyle below what you can afford is avoiding the psychological treadmill of keeping up with the Joneses. Comfortably living below what you can afford, without much desire for more, removes a tremendous amount of social pressure that many people in the modern first world subject themselves to. Nassim Taleb explained: "True success is exiting some rat race to modulate one's activities for peace of mind." I like that.

We're so far committed to the independence camp that we've done things that make little sense on paper. We own our house without a mortgage, which is the worst financial decision we've ever made but the best money decision we've ever made. Mortgage interest rates were absurdly low when we bought our house. Any rational advisor would recommend taking advantage of cheap money and investing extra savings in higher-return assets, like stocks. But our goal isn't to be coldly rational; just psychologically reasonable.

The independent feeling I get from owning our house outright far exceeds the known financial gain I'd get from leveraging our assets with a cheap mortgage. Eliminating the monthly payment feels better than maximizing the long-term value of our assets. It makes me feel independent.

I don't try to defend this decision to those pointing out its flaws, or those who would never do the same. On paper it's defenseless. But it works for us. We like it. That's what matters. Good decisions aren't always rational. At some point you have to choose between being happy or being "right."

We also keep a higher percentage of our assets in cash than most financial advisors would recommend—something around 20% of our assets outside the value of our house. This is also close to indefensible on paper, and I'm not recommending it to others. It's just what works for us.

We do it because cash is the oxygen of independence, and—more importantly—we never want to be forced to sell the stocks we own. We want the probability of facing a huge expense and needing to liquidate stocks to cover it to be as close to zero as possible. Perhaps we just have a lower risk tolerance than others.

But everything I've learned about personal finance tells me that everyone—without exception—will eventually face a huge expense they did not expect—and they don't plan for these expenses specifically because they did not expect them. The few people who know the details of our finances ask, "What are you saving for? A house? A boat? A new car?" No, none of those. I'm saving for a world where curveballs are more common than we expect. Not being forced to sell stocks to cover an expense also means we're increasing the odds of letting the stocks we own compound for the longest period of time. Charlie Munger put it well: "The first rule of compounding is to never interrupt it unnecessarily."

How my family thinks about investing

I started my career as a stock picker. At the time we only owned individual stocks, mostly large companies like Berkshire Hathaway and Procter & Gamble, mixed with smaller stocks I considered deep value investments. Go back to my 20s and at any given point I held something like 25 individual stocks.

I don't know how I did as a stock picker. Did I beat the market? I'm not sure. Like most who try, I didn't keep a good score. Either way, I've shifted my views and now every stock we own is a low-cost index fund.

I don't have anything against actively picking stocks, either on your own or through giving your money to an active fund manager. I think some people can outperform the market averages—it's just very hard, and harder than most people think.

If I had to summarize my views on investing, it's this: Every investor should pick a strategy that has the highest odds of successfully meeting their goals. And I think for most investors, dollar-cost averaging into a low-cost index fund will provide the highest odds of long-term success.

That doesn't mean index investing will always work. It doesn't mean it's for everyone. And it doesn't mean active stock picking is doomed to fail. In general, this industry has become too entrenched on one side or the other—particularly those vehemently against active investing.

Beating the market *should be hard*; the odds of success *should be low*. If they weren't, everyone would do it, and if everyone did it there would be no opportunity. So no one should be surprised that the majority of those trying to beat the market fail to do so. (The statistics show 85% of large-cap active managers didn't beat the S&P 500 over the decade ending 2019.)[71]

I know people who think it's insane to try to beat the market but encourage their kids to reach for the stars and try to become professional athletes. To each their own. Life is about playing the odds, and we all think about odds a little differently.

Over the years I came around to the view that we'll have a high chance of meeting all of our family's financial goals if we consistently invest money into a low-cost index fund for decades on end, leaving the money alone to compound. A lot of this view comes from our lifestyle of frugal spending. If you can meet all your goals without having to take the added risk that comes from trying to outperform the market, then what's the point of even trying? I can afford to not be the greatest investor in the world, but I can't afford to be a bad one. When I think of it that way, the choice to buy the index and hold on is a no-brainer for us. I know not everyone will agree with that logic, especially my friends whose job it is to beat the market. I respect what they do. But this is what works for us.

We invest money from every paycheck into these index funds—a combination of U.S. and international stocks. There's no set goal—it's just whatever is leftover after we spend. We max out retirement accounts in the same funds, and contribute to our kids' 529 college savings plans.

And that's about it. Effectively all of our net worth is a house, a checking account, and some Vanguard index funds.

It doesn't need to be more complicated than that for us. I like it simple. One of my deeply held investing beliefs is that there is little correlation between investment effort and investment results. The reason is because the world is driven by tails—a few variables account for the majority of returns. No matter how hard you try at investing you won't do well if you miss the two or three things that move the needle in your strategy. The reverse is true. Simple investment strategies can work great as long as they capture the few things that are important to that strategy's success. My investing strategy doesn't rely on picking the right sector, or timing the next recession. It relies on a high savings rate, patience, and optimism that the global economy will create value over the next several decades. I spend virtually all of my investing effort thinking about those three things—especially the first two, which I can control.

I've changed my investment strategy in the past. So of course there's a chance I'll change it in the future.

No matter how we save or invest I'm sure we'll always have the goal of independence, and we'll always do whatever maximizes for sleeping well at night.

We think it's the ultimate goal; the mastery of the psychology of money.

But to each their own. No one is crazy.

POSTSCRIPT: A Brief History of Why the U.S. Consumer Thinks the Way They Do

To understand the psychology of the modern consumer and to grasp where they might be heading next, you have to know how they got here.

How *we all* got here.

If you fell asleep in 1945 and woke up in 2020 you would not recognize the world around you.

The amount of economic growth that took place during that period is virtually unprecedented. If you saw the level of wealth in New York and San Francisco, you'd be shocked. If you compared it to the poverty of Detroit, you'd be shocked. If you saw the price of homes, college tuition, and health care, you'd be shocked. If you saw how average Americans think about savings and spending in general, you'd be shocked. And if you tried to think of a reasonable narrative of how it all happened, my guess is you'd be totally wrong. Because it isn't intuitive, and it wasn't foreseeable.

What happened in America since the end of World War II is

the story of the American consumer. It's a story that helps explain why people think about money the way they do today.

The short story is this: Things were very uncertain, then they were very good, then pretty bad, then really good, then really bad, and now here we are. And there is, I think, a narrative that links all those events together. Not a detailed account. But a story of how things fit together.

Since this is an attempt to link the big events together, it leaves out many details of what happened during this period. I'm likely to agree with anyone who points out what I've missed. The goal here is not to describe every play; it's to look at how one game influenced the next.

Here's how the modern consumer got here.

---

1. August, 1945. World War II ends.

Japan surrendering was "The Happiest Day in American History," *The New York Times* wrote.

But there's the saying, "History is just one damn thing after another."

The joy of the war ending was quickly met with the question, "What happens now?"

Sixteen million Americans—11% of the population—served in the war. About eight million were overseas at the end. Their average age was 23. Within 18 months all but 1.5 million of them would be home and out of uniform.

And then what?

What were they going to do next?

Where were they going to work?

Where were they going to live?

Those were the most important questions of the day, for two

reasons. One, no one knew the answers. Two, if they couldn't be answered quickly, the most likely scenario—in the eyes of many economists—was that the economy would slip back into the depths of the Great Depression.

Three forces had built up during the war:

1. Housing construction ground to a halt, as virtually all production capacity was shifted to building war supplies. Fewer than 12,000 homes per month were built in 1943, equivalent to less than one new home per American city. Returning soldiers faced a severe housing shortage.
2. The specific jobs created during the war—building ships, tanks, and planes—were very suddenly not necessary after it, stopping with a speed and magnitude rarely seen in private business. It was unclear where soldiers could work.
3. The marriage rate spiked during and immediately after the war. Soldiers didn't want to return to their mother's basement. They wanted to start a family, in their own home, with a good job, right away.

This worried policymakers, especially since the Great Depression was still a recent memory, having ended just five years prior.

In 1946 the Council of Economic Advisors delivered a report to President Truman warning of "a full-scale depression some time in the next one to four years."

They wrote in a separate 1947 memo, summarizing a meeting with Truman:

> We might be in some sort of recession period where we should have to be very sure of our ground as to whether recessionary forces might be in danger of getting out of hand ... There is a substantial prospect which should not be overlooked that a further decline may increase the danger of a downward spiral into depression conditions.

This fear was exacerbated by the fact that exports couldn't be immediately relied upon for growth, as two of the largest economies—Europe and Japan—sat in ruins dealing with humanitarian crises. And America itself was buried in more debt than ever before, limiting direct government stimulus.

So we did something about it.

2. Low interest rates and the intentional birth of the American consumer.

The first thing we did to keep the economy afloat after the war was keep interest rates low. This wasn't an easy decision, because when soldiers came home to a shortage of everything from clothes to cars it temporarily sent inflation into double digits.

The Federal Reserve was not politically independent before 1951.[72] The president and the Fed could coordinate policy. In 1942 the Fed announced it would keep short-term rates at 0.38% to help finance the war. Rates didn't budge a single basis point for the next seven years. Three-month Treasury yields stayed below 2% until the mid-1950s.

The explicit reason for keeping rates down was to keep the cost of financing the equivalent of the $6 trillion we spent on the war low.

But low rates also did something else for all the returning GIs. It made borrowing to buy homes, cars, gadgets, and toys really cheap.

Which, from a paranoid policymaker's perspective, was great. Consumption became an explicit economic strategy in the years after World War II.

An era of encouraging thrift and saving to fund the war quickly turned into an era of actively promoting spending. Princeton historian Sheldon Garon writes:

> After 1945, America again diverged from patterns of savings promotion in Europe and East Asia ... Politicians, businessmen and labor leaders all encouraged Americans to spend to foster economic growth.[73]

Two things fueled this push.

One was the GI Bill, which offered unprecedented mortgage opportunities. Sixteen million veterans could buy a home often with no money down, no interest in the first year, and fixed rates so low that monthly mortgage payments could be lower than a rental.

The second was an explosion of consumer credit, enabled by the loosening of Depression-era regulations. The first credit card was introduced in 1950. Store credit, installment credit, personal loans, payday loans—everything took off. And interest on all debt, including credit cards, was tax deductible at the time.

It tasted delicious. So we ate a lot of it. A simple story in a simple table:

Year	Total US Household Debt
1945	$29.4 billion
1955	$125.7 billion
1965	$331.2 billion

Household debt in the 1950s grew 1.5 times faster than it did during the 2000s debt splurge.

3. Pent-up demand for stuff fed by a credit boom and a hidden 1930s productivity boom led to an economic boom.

The 1930s were the hardest economic decade in American history. But there was a silver lining that took two decades to notice: By necessity, the Great Depression had supercharged resourcefulness, productivity, and innovation.

We didn't pay that much attention to the productivity boom in the '30s, because everyone was focused on how bad the economy was. We didn't pay attention to it in the '40s, because everyone was focused on the war.

Then the 1950s came around and we suddenly realized, "Wow, we have some amazing new inventions. And we're really good at making them."

Appliances, cars, phones, air conditioning, electricity.

It was nearly impossible to buy many household goods during the war, because factories were converted to make guns and ships. That created pent-up demand from GIs for stuff after the war ended. Married, eager to get on with life, and emboldened with new cheap consumer credit, they went on a buying spree like the country had never seen.

Frederick Lewis Allen writes in his book *The Big Change*:

> During these postwar years the farmer bought a new tractor, a corn picker, an electric milking machine; in fact he and his neighbors, between them, assembled a formidable array of farm machinery for their joint use. The farmer's wife got the shining white electric refrigerator she had always longed for and never during the Great Depression had been able to afford, and an up-to-date washing machine, and a deep-freeze unit. The suburban family installed a dishwashing machine and invested in a power lawnmower. The city family became customers of a laundromat and acquired a television set for the living room. The husband's office was air-conditioned. And so on endlessly.

It's hard to overstate how big this surge was.

Commercial car and truck manufacturing virtually ceased from 1942 to 1945. Then 21 million cars were sold from 1945 to 1949. Another 37 million were sold by 1955.

Just under two million homes were built from 1940 to 1945. Then seven million were built from 1945 to 1950. Another eight million were built by 1955.

Pent-up demand for stuff, and our newfound ability to make stuff, created the jobs that put returning GIs back to work. And they were good jobs, too. Mix that with consumer credit, and America's capacity for spending exploded.

The Federal Reserve wrote to President Truman in 1951: "By 1950, total consumer expenditures, together with residential construction, amounted to about 203 billion dollars, or in the neighborhood of 40 percent above the 1944 level."[74]

The answer to the question, "What are all these GIs going to do after the war?" was now obvious. They were going to buy stuff, with money earned from their jobs making new stuff, helped by cheap borrowed money to buy even more stuff.

4. Gains are shared more equally than ever before.

The defining characteristic of economics in the 1950s is that the country got rich by making the poor less poor.

Average wages doubled from 1940 to 1948, then doubled again by 1963.

And those gains focused on those who had been left behind for decades before. The gap between rich and poor narrowed by an extraordinary amount.

Lewis Allen wrote in 1955:

> The enormous lead of the well-to-do in the economic race has been considerably reduced.
>
> It is the industrial workers who as a group have done best—people such as a steelworker's family who used to live on $2,500 and now are getting $4,500, or the highly skilled machine-tool operator's family who used to have $3,000 and now can spend an annual $5,500 or more.
>
> As for the top one percent, the really well-to-do and the rich, whom we might classify very roughly indeed as the

> $16,000-and-over group, their share of the total national income, after taxes, had come down by 1945 from 13 percent to 7 percent.

This was not a short-term trend. Real income for the bottom 20% of wage-earners grew by a nearly identical amount as the top 5% from 1950 to 1980.

The equality went beyond wages.

Women held jobs outside the home in record numbers. Their labor force participation rate went from 31% after the war to 37% by 1955, and to 40% by 1965.

Minorities gained, too. After the 1945 inauguration Eleanor Roosevelt wrote about an African American reporter who told her:

> Do you realize what twelve years have done? If at the 1933 reception a number of colored people had gone down the line and mixed with everyone else in the way they did today, every paper in the country would have reported it. We do not even think it is news and none of us will mention it.

Women and minority rights were still a fraction of what they are today. But the progress toward equality in the late '40s and '50s was extraordinary.

The leveling out of classes meant a leveling out of lifestyles. Normal people drove Chevys. Rich people drove Cadillacs. TV and radio equalized the entertainment and culture people enjoyed regardless of class. Mail-order catalogs equalized the clothes people wore and the goods they bought regardless of where they lived. *Harper's Magazine* noted in 1957:

> The rich man smokes the same sort of cigarettes as the poor man, shaves with the same sort of razor, uses the same sort of telephone, vacuum cleaner, radio, and TV set, has the same sort of lighting and heating equipment in his house, and so on indefinitely. The

> differences between his automobile and the poor man's are minor. Essentially they have similar engines, similar fittings. In the early years of the century there was a hierarchy of automobiles.

Paul Graham wrote in 2016 about what something as simple as there only being three TV stations did to equalize culture:

> It's difficult to imagine now, but every night tens of millions of families would sit down together in front of their TV set watching the same show, at the same time, as their next door neighbors. What happens now with the Super Bowl used to happen every night. We were literally in sync.[75]

This was important. People measure their well-being against their peers. And for most of the 1945–1980 period, people had a lot of what looked like peers to compare themselves to. Many people—most people—lived lives that were either equal or at least fathomable to those around them. The idea that people's lives equalized as much as their incomes is an important point of this story we'll come back to.

5. Debt rose tremendously. But so did incomes, so the impact wasn't a big deal.

Household debt increased fivefold from 1947 to 1957 due to the combination of the new consumption culture, new debt products, and interest rates subsidized by government programs, and held low by the Federal Reserve.

But income growth was so strong during this period that the impact on households wasn't severe. And household debt was so low to begin with after the war. The Great Depression wiped out a lot of it, and household spending was so curtailed during the war that debt accumulation was restricted. So the growth in household debt-to-income from 1947–1957 was manageable.

Household debt-to-income today is just over 100%. Even after rising in the 1950s, 1960s, and 1970s, it stayed below 60%.

Driving a lot of this debt boom was a surge in home ownership. The homeownership rate in 1900 was 47%. It stayed right about there for the next four decades. Then it took off, hitting 53% by 1945 and 62% by 1970. A substantial portion of the population was now using debt that previous generations would not—could not—have accessed. And they were mostly OK with it.

David Halberstam writes in his book *The Fifties*:

> They were confident in themselves and their futures in a way that [those] growing up in harder times found striking. They did not fear debt as their parents had ... They differed from their parents not just in how much they made and what they owned but in their belief that the future had already arrived. As the first homeowners in their families, they brought a new excitement and pride with them to the store as they bought furniture or appliances—in other times young couples might have exhibited such feelings as they bought clothes for their first baby. It was as if the very accomplishment of owning a home reflected such an immense breakthrough that nothing was too good to buy for it.

Now's a good time to connect a few things, as they'll become increasingly important:

- America is booming.
- It's booming *together* like never before.
- It's booming with debt that isn't a big deal at the time because it's still low relative to income and there's a cultural acceptance that debt isn't a scary thing.

6. Things start cracking.

1973 was the first year where it became clear the economy was walking down a new path.

The recession that began that year brought unemployment to the highest it had been since the 1930s.

Inflation surged. But unlike the post-war spikes, it stayed high.

Short-term interest rates hit 8% in 1973, up from 2.5% a decade earlier.

And you have to put all of that in the context of how much fear there was between Vietnam, riots, and the assassinations of Martin Luther King, and John and Bobby Kennedy.

It got bleak.

America dominated the world economy in the two decades after the war. Many of the largest countries had their manufacturing capacity bombed into rubble. But as the 1970s emerged, that changed. Japan was booming. China's economy was opening up. The Middle East was flexing its oil muscles.

A combination of lucky economic advantages and a culture shared by the Greatest Generation—hardened by the Depression and anchored in systematic cooperation from the war—shifted when Baby Boomers began coming of age. A new generation that had a different view of what's normal hit at the same time a lot of the economic tailwinds of the previous two decades ended.

Everything in finance is data *within the context of expectations.* One of the biggest shifts of the last century happened when the economic winds began blowing in a different, uneven direction, but people's expectations were still rooted in a post-war culture of equality. Not necessarily equality of income, although there was that. But equality in lifestyle and consumption expectations; the idea that someone earning a 50th percentile income shouldn't live a life dramatically different than someone in the 80th or 90th percentile. And that someone in the 99th percentile lived a better life, but still a life that someone in the 50th percentile could comprehend. That's how America worked for most of the 1945–1980 period. It doesn't matter whether you think that's morally right or wrong. It just matters that it happened.

Expectations always move slower than facts. And the economic facts of the years between the early 1970s through the early 2000s were that growth continued, but became more uneven, yet people's expectations of how their lifestyle should compare to their peers did not change.

7. The boom resumes, but it's different than before.

Ronald Reagan's 1984 "Morning in America" ad declared:

> It's morning again in America. Today more men and women will go to work than ever before in our country's history. With interest rates at about half the record highs of 1980, nearly 2,000 families today will buy new homes, more than at any time in the past four years. This afternoon 6,500 young men and women will be married, and with inflation at less than half of what it was just four years ago, they can look forward with confidence to the future.

That wasn't hyperbole. GDP growth was the highest it had been since the 1950s. By 1989 there were six million fewer unemployed Americans than there were seven years before. The S&P 500 rose almost fourfold between 1982 and 1990. Total real GDP growth in the 1990s was roughly equal to that of the 1950s—40% vs. 42%.

President Clinton boasted in his 2000 State of the Union speech:

> We begin the new century with over 20 million new jobs; the fastest economic growth in more than 30 years; the lowest unemployment rates in 30 years; the lowest poverty

> rates in 20 years; the lowest African-American and Hispanic unemployment rates on record; the first back-to-back surpluses in 42 years; and next month, America will achieve the longest period of economic growth in our entire history. We have built a new economy.

His last sentence was important. It was a *new* economy. The biggest difference between the economy of the 1945–1973 period and that of the 1982–2000 period was that the same amount of growth found its way into totally different pockets.

You've probably heard these numbers but they're worth rehashing. *The Atlantic* writes:

> Between 1993 and 2012, the top 1 percent saw their incomes grow 86.1 percent, while the bottom 99 percent saw just 6.6 percent growth.

Joseph Stiglitz in 2011:

> While the top 1 percent have seen their incomes rise 18 percent over the past decade, those in the middle have actually seen their incomes fall. For men with only high-school degrees, the decline has been precipitous—12 percent in the last quarter-century alone.

It was nearly the opposite of the flattening that occurred after the war.

Why this happened is one of the nastiest debates in economics, topped only by the debate over what we should do about it. Lucky for the purpose of this discussion, neither matters.

All that matters is that sharp inequality became a force over the last 35 years, and it happened during a period where, culturally, Americans held onto two ideas rooted in the post-WW2 economy: That you should live a lifestyle similar to most other Americans, and that taking on debt to finance that lifestyle is acceptable.

8. The big stretch.

Rising incomes among a small group of Americans led to that group breaking away in lifestyle.

They bought bigger homes, nicer cars, went to expensive schools, and took fancy vacations.

And everyone else was watching—fueled by Madison Avenue in the '80s and '90s, and the internet after that.

The lifestyles of a small portion of legitimately rich Americans inflated the aspirations of the majority of Americans, whose incomes weren't rising.

A culture of equality and togetherness that came out of the 1950s–1970s innocently morphs into a Keeping Up With The Joneses effect.

Now you can see the problem.

Joe, an investment banker making $900,000 a year, buys a 4,000 square foot house with two Mercedes and sends three of his kids to Pepperdine. He can afford it.

Peter, a bank branch manager making $80,000 a year, sees Joe and feels a subconscious sense of entitlement to live a similar lifestyle, because Peter's parents believed—and instilled in him—that Americans' lifestyles weren't that different even if they had different jobs. His parents were right during their era, because incomes fell into a tight distribution. But that was then. Peter lives in a different world. But his expectations haven't changed much from his parents', even if the facts have.

So what does Peter do?

He takes out a huge mortgage. He has $45,000 of credit card debt. He leases two cars. His kids will graduate with heavy student loans. He can't afford the stuff Joe can, but he's pushed to stretch for the same lifestyle. It is a big stretch.

This would have seemed preposterous to someone in the 1930s.

But we've spent 75 years since the end of the war fostering a cultural acceptance of household debt.

During a time when median wages were flat, the median new American home grew 50% larger.

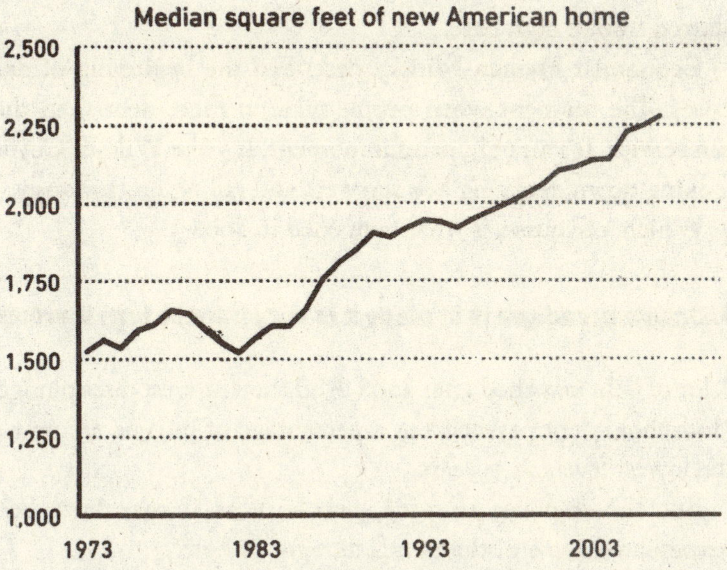

The average new American home now has more bathrooms than occupants. Nearly half have four or more bedrooms, up from 18% in 1983.

The average car loan adjusted for inflation more than doubled between 1975 and 2003, from $12,300 to $27,900.

And you know what happened to college costs and student loans.

Household debt-to-income stayed about flat from 1963 to 1973. Then it climbed, and climbed, and climbed, from around 60% in 1973 to more than 130% by 2007.

Even as interest rates plunged from the early 1980s through 2020, the percentage of income going to debt service payments rose. And it skewed toward lower-income groups. The share of income going toward debt and lease payments is just over 8% for the highest income groups—those with the biggest income gains—but over 21% for those below the 50th percentile.

The difference between this climbing debt and the debt increase that took place during the 1950s and '60s is that the recent jump started from a high base.

Economist Hyman Minsky described the beginning of debt crises: The moment when people take on more debt than they can service. It's an ugly, painful moment. It's like Wile E. Coyote looking down, realizing he's screwed, and falling precipitously.

Which, of course, is what happened in 2008.

9. Once a paradigm is in place it is very hard to turn it around.

A lot of debt was shed after 2008. And then interest rates plunged. Household debt payments as a percentage of income are now at the lowest levels in 35 years.

But the response to 2008, necessary as it may have been, perpetuated some of the trends that got us here.

Quantitative easing both prevented economic collapse and boosted asset prices, a boon for those who owned them—mostly rich people.

The Fed backstopped corporate debt in 2008. That helped those who owned that debt—mostly rich people.

Tax cuts over the last 20 years have predominantly gone to those with higher incomes. People with higher incomes send their kids to the best colleges. Those kids can go on to earn higher incomes and invest in corporate debt that will be backstopped by the Fed, own stocks that will be supported by various government policies, and so on.

None of these things are problems in and of themselves, which is why they stay in place.

But they're symptomatic of the bigger thing that's happened

since the early 1980s: The economy works better for some people than others. Success isn't as meritocratic as it used to be and, when success is granted, it's rewarded with higher gains than in previous eras.

You don't have to think that's morally right or wrong.

And, again, in this story it doesn't matter why it happened.

It just matters *that it did happen*, and it caused the economy to shift away from people's expectations that were set after the war: That there's a broad middle class without systematic inequality, where your neighbors next door and a few miles down the road live a life that's pretty similar to yours.

Part of the reason these expectations have stuck around for 35 years after they shifted away from reality is because they felt so good for so many people when they were valid. Something that good—or at least the impression that it was that good—isn't easy to let go of.

So people haven't let go of it. They want it back.

10. The Tea Party, Occupy Wall Street, Brexit, and Donald Trump each represents a group shouting, "Stop the ride, I want off."

The details of their shouting are different, but they're all shouting—at least in part—because stuff isn't working for them within the context of the post war expectation that stuff should work roughly the same for roughly everyone.

You can scoff at linking the rise of Trump to income inequality alone. And you should. These things are always layers of complexity deep. But it's a key part of what drives people to think, "I don't live in the world I expected. That pisses me off. So screw this. And screw you! I'm going to fight for something totally different, because this—whatever it is—isn't working."

Take that mentality and raise it to the power of Facebook,

Instagram, and cable news—where people are more keenly aware of how other people live than ever before. It's gasoline on a flame. Benedict Evans says, "The more the Internet exposes people to new points of view, the angrier people get that different views exist." That's a big shift from the post-war economy where the range of economic opinions were smaller, both because the actual range of outcomes was lower and because it wasn't as easy to see and learn what other people thought and how they lived.

I'm not pessimistic. Economics is the story of cycles. Things come, things go.

The unemployment rate is now the lowest it's been in decades. Wages are now actually growing faster for low-income workers than the rich.[76] College costs by and large stopped growing once grants are factored in.[77] If everyone studied advances in health care, communication, transportation, and civil rights since the Glorious 1950s, my guess is most wouldn't want to go back.

But a central theme of this story is that expectations move slower than reality on the ground. That was true when people clung to 1950s expectations as the economy changed over the next 35 years. And even if a middle-class boom began today, expectations that the odds are stacked against everyone but those at the top may stick around.

So the era of "This isn't working" may stick around.

And the era of "We need something radically new, right now, whatever it is" may stick around.

Which, in a way, is part of what starts events that led to things like World War II, where this story began.

History is just one damned thing after another.

Endnotes

1 J. Pressler, "Former Merrill Lynch Executive Forced to Declare Bankruptcy Just to Keep a $14 Million Roof Over His Head," *New York* magazine (April 9, 2010).

2 Ibid.

3 L. Thomas Jr., "The Tale of the $8 Million 'Bargain' House in Greenwich," *The New York Times* (January 25, 2014).

4 U. Malmendier, S. Nagel, "Depression Babies: Do Macroeconomic Experiences Affect Risk-Taking?" (August 2007).

5 "How large are 401(k)s?" Investment Company Institute (December 2019).

6 R. Butler, "Retirement Pay Often Is Scanty," *The New York Times* (August 14, 1955).

7 "Higher education in the United States," Wikipedia.

8 K. Bancalari, "Private college tuition is rising faster than inflation .... again," *USA Today* (June 9, 2017).

9 "How Many People Die Rock Climbing?" The Rockulus.

10 A. T. Vanderbilt II, *Fortune's Children: The Fall of the House of Vanderbilt* (William Morrow Paperbacks, 2012).

11 D. McDonald, "Rajat Gupta: Touched by scandal," *Fortune* (October 1, 2010).

12 "Did millionaire Rajat Gupta suffer from billionaire envy?" *The Economic Times* (March 27, 2011).

13 J. Nicas, "Facebook Connected Her to a Tattooed Soldier in Iraq. Or So She Thought," *The New York Times* (July 28, 2019).

14 T. Maloney, "The Best-Paid Hedge Fund Managers Made $7.7 Billion in 2018," Bloomberg (February 15, 2019).

15 S. Weart, "The Discovery of Global Warming," history.aip.org/climate/cycles.htm (January 2020).

16 S. Langlois, "From $6,000 to $73 billion: Warren Buffett's wealth through the ages," MarketWatch (January 6, 2017).

17 D. Boudreaux, "Turnover in the Forbes 400, 2008–2013," Cafe Hayek (May 16, 2014).

18 M. Pabrai, www.youtube.com/watch?time_continue=200&v=YmmIbrKDYbw.

19 "Art Dealers: The Other Vincent van Gogh," Horizon Research Group (June 2010).

20 www.collaborativefund.com/uploads/venture-returns.png

21 "The Agony and the Ecstasy: The Risks and Rewards of a Concentrated Stock Position," Eye on the Market, J.P. Morgan (2014).

22 L. Eadicicco, "Here's Why You Probably Won't Get Hired At Google," Business Insider (October 23, 2014).

23 "What is the offer acceptance rate for Facebook software engineering positions?" Quora.com.
24 W. Fulton, "If You Want to Build a Great Team, Hire Apple Employees," *Forbes* (June 22, 2012).
25 J. Berger, "How to Change Anyone's Mind," *The Wall Street Journal* (February 21, 2020).
26 D. Sivers, "How I got rich on the other hand," sivers.org (October 30, 2019).
27 N. Chokshi, "Americans Are Among the Most Stressed People in the World, Poll Finds," *The New York Times* (April 25, 2019).
28 Russell Sage Foundation—Chartbook of Social Inequality.
29 D. Thompson, "Why White-Collar Workers Spend All Day at the Office," *The Atlantic* (December 4, 2019).
30 "Rihanna's ex-accountant fires back," News24 (March 24, 2014).
31 B. Mann, "Want to Get Rich and Stay Rich?" The Motley Fool (March 7, 2017).
32 "U.S. energy intensity projected to continue its steady decline through 2040," U.S. Energy Information Administration (March 1, 2013).
33 Julius Wagner-Jauregg—Biographical, nobelprize.org.
34 J. M. Cavaillon, "Good and bad fever," *Critical Care* 16:2 (2012).
35 "Fever—Myths Versus Facts," Seattle Children's.
36 J. J. Ray, and C. I. Schulman, "Fever: suppress or let it ride?" *Journal of Thoracic Disease* 7:12 (2015).
37 A. LaFrance, "A Cultural History of the Fever," *The Atlantic* (September 16, 2015).
38 J. Zweig, "What Harry Markowitz Meant," jasonzweig.com (October 2, 2017).
39 L. Pleven, "In Bogle Family, It's Either Passive or Aggressive," *The Wall Street Journal* (November 28, 2013).
40 C. Shapiro and M. Housel, "Disrupting Investors' Own Game," The Collaborative Fund.
41 www.bylo.org
42 Washington State University, "For pundits, it's better to be confident than correct," ScienceDaily (May 28, 2013).
43 "Daniel Kahneman's Favorite Approach For Making Better Decisions," Farnham Street (January 2014).
44 W. Buffett, Letter to the Shareholders of Berkshire Hathaway Inc. (2008).
45 W. Buffett, Letter to the Shareholders of Berkshire Hathaway Inc. (2006).
46 B. Plumer, "Only 27 percent of college grads have a job related to their major," *The Washington Post* (May 20, 2013).
47 G. Livingston, "Stay-at-home moms and dads account for about one-in-five U.S. parents," Pew Research Center (September 24, 2018).
48 D. Gilbert, "The psychology of your future self," TED2014.
49 J. Zweig, "What I Learned From Daniel Kahneman," jasonzweig.com (March 30, 2014).
50 J. Ptak "Tactical Funds Miss Their Chance," Morningstar (February 2, 2012).
51 R. Kinnel, "Mind the Gap 2019," Morningstar (August 15, 2019).
52 M. Desmond. "Accounting Tricks Catch Up With GE," *Forbes* (August 4, 2009).

53 A. Berenson, "Freddie Mac Says It Understated Profits by Up to $6.9 Billion," *The New York Times* (June 25, 2003).

54 "U.S. Home Flipping Rate Reaches a Nine-Year High in Q1 2019," Attom Data Solutions (June 4, 2019).

55 A. Osborn, "As if Things Weren't Bad Enough, Russian Professor Predicts End of U.S.," *The Wall Street Journal* (December 29, 2008).

56 "Food in the Occupation of Japan," Wikipedia.

57 J. M. Jones, "U.S. Stock Ownership Down Among All but Older, Higher-Income," Gallup (May 27, 2017).

58 E. Rauchway, *The Great Depression and the New Deal: A Very Short Introduction* (Oxford University Press, 2008).

59 L. R. Brown, *Plan B 3.0: Mobilizing to Save Civilization* (W. W. Norton & Company, 2008).

60 FRED, Federal Reserve Bank of St. Louis.

61 "U.S. Crude Oil Production—Historical Chart," Macro Trends.

62 "Thomas Selfridge," Wikipedia.

63 www.nhlbi.nih.gov

64 D. Walsh, "The Tragedy of Saudi Arabia's War," *The New York Times* (October 26, 2018).

65 B. Pisani, "Active fund managers trail the S&P 500 for the ninth year in a row in triumph for indexing," CNBC (March 15, 2019).

66 *2019 Investment Company Factbook*, Investment Company Institute.

67 "Minutes of the Federal Open Market Committee," Federal Reserve (October 30–31, 2007).

68 www.nasa.gov

69 A. Ram, "Portfolio managers shun investing in own funds," *Financial Times* (September 18, 2016).

70 K. Murray "How Doctors Die," Zócalo Public Square (November 30, 2011).

71 B. Pisani, "Active fund managers trail the S&P 500 for the ninth year in a row in triumph for indexing," CNBC (March 15, 2019).

72 "Treasury-Fed Accord," federalreservehistory.org.

73 S. Garon, "Beyond Our Means: Why America Spends While the World Saves," Federal Reserve Bank of St. Louis (July 1, 2012).

74 "Economic Report of the President," FRASER, St. Louis Federal Reserve (1951).

75 P. Graham, "The Refragmentation," paulgraham.com (2016).

76 P. Davidson, "Jobs in high-wage industries are growing fastest," *USA Today* (December 14, 2019).

77 R. Channick, "Average college costs flat nationwide, at just under $15K, as universities increase grants," *Chicago Tribune* (October 16, 2018).

Acknowledgements

Like all books, *The Psychology of Money* wouldn't have been possible without the help of countless people who helped me along the way. There are too many to list them all. But a few who have been particularly supportive:

Brian Richards, who bet on me before anyone else.

Craig Shapiro, who bet on me when he didn't have to.

Gretchen Housel, whose support is unwavering.

Jenna Abdou, who helps while asking for nothing in return.

Craig Pearce, who encourages, guides, and grounds me.

Jamie Catherwood, Josh Brown, Brent Beshore, Barry Ritholtz, Ben Carlson, Chris Hill, Michael Batnick, James Osorne, whose feedback is invaluable.

Thank you.